Poetry Ireland Review 128

Eagarthóir / Editor
EAVAN BOLAND

Poetry Ireland Ltd/Éigse Éireann Teo gratefully acknowledges the assistance of
The Arts Council/An Chomhairle Ealaíon and The Arts Council of Northern Ireland.

LOTTERY FUNDED

Poetry Ireland invites individuals and commercial organizations to become
Friends of Poetry Ireland. For more details, please contact:
Poetry Ireland Friends Scheme, Poetry Ireland, 11 Parnell Square East,
Dublin 1, Ireland
or telephone +353 1 6789815; e-mail info@poetryireland.ie

FOUNDING PARTNERS
Adrian Brinkerhoff Poetry Fund of the Sidney E Frank Foundation
University College Cork

POETRY PATRONS: EPIC
Thomas Dillon Redshaw

POETRY PATRONS: LYRIC
Eithne Hand, Ruth Webster

POETRY PATRONS: SONNET
Neville Keery, Nana Lampton, William McConkey, Joan and Joe McBreen, Anonymous

POETRY PATRON: HAIKU
Ciara McCluskey

FRIENDS OF POETRY IRELAND
Desmond Windle, Rachel Joynt, Noel and Anne Monahan, Maurice Earls, Mary Shine
Thompson, Seán Coyle, Andrew Caldicott, Henry and Deirdre Comerford

Poetry Ireland Review is published three times a year by Poetry Ireland Ltd. The Editor
enjoys complete autonomy in the choice of material published. The contents of this
publication should not be taken to reflect either the views or the policy of the publishers.

ISBN: 978-1-902121-77-2   ISSN: 0332-2998

PUBLICATIONS MANAGER: Paul Lenehan and Rachel Botha, with the assistance of
Alexandria Andrews, Eoin Rogers, and Orla Higgins

IRISH-LANGUAGE EDITOR: Caitríona Ní Chléirchín
DESIGN: Alistair Keady (www.hexhibit.com)
COVER CREDIT: *Derek and his Dog on Top of the Silage Pit* (2017) by Ann Quinn

Contents

Poetry Ireland Review 128

Editorial

In the early 1940's the Russian poet, Anna Akhmatova, was writing her elegy 'Requiem'. It recorded the grief and dispossession of the Stalin purges. It was also a dangerous enterprise. She feared the secret police, the discovery of her manuscript, and what might follow.

Her solution was makeshift and workable. She wrote down fragments. She gave them to friends. Her friends memorised them. Then the paper was burned. Her friend Lydia Chukovskaya, a poet and dissident, was one of those who helped. "It was like a ritual," she later recalled. "Hands, matches, an ashtray. A ritual beautiful and bitter."

In 2007, at the Hay Festival, the distinguished novelist Martin Amis gave another view. "You may have noticed that poetry is dead." he said. "The obituary has already been written ... I mean, it goes on, and its funny, ghoulish afterlife is in the form of tours and readings and poetry slams and all the rest of it, but not many people now curl up in the evening with a book of poetry."

Those passionate, chosen friends of Anna Akhmatova were certainly not living a so-called ghoulish afterlife. They lived in a knife-edge present. In that space they may have doubted their survival under a regime which confused poets with enemies of the state. But they did not doubt the life of poetry. They lent to it their own memories, their own belief that the words they memorised were necessary. They lent to it their courage and their faith in an essential art.

These events and opinions are separated by decades, What happened in between? One answer lies in the argument that a powerful popular culture, with its emphasis on dailyness and details, turned out to be no ally of a great and complex art. Martin Amis's views could not have been given a hundred years earlier, maybe not even fifty years earlier. But in the moment he offered them, for some people at least, poetry seemed to be in the shadows: its language and existence still vital to many, but its place in their culture and society poorly defined.

With the heavy contrast between these actions and statements, an emerging poet might well feel less than comfortable with the present state of things. The art they practice may seem called into question too often. They might also ask – is there a remedy? Is there something a new poet can do, or an established one, to take on the challenges of their time and engage with the questions around them?

I think there is. The remedy lies in the very shift that has occurred over the past decades. Once a poet was thought of as solitary, as closed in a private world. As a vendor of private perceptions and visions. That solitude was a source of esteem in the outside world. But a great deal has changed. Now poets are able to draw some part of their identity from the communal, the public, the gathering places – from panels to performance – which reinforce their identity and make visible their purpose .

Nor are such communities makeshift or temporary. Poetry Ireland has provided a remarkable community for decades, together with innovative ideas on how to strengthen it and sustain it. The Poetry Foundation and the Academy of American Poets in the US have the same purpose. If a popular culture was no help to the art, the digital age has proved to be the opposite: providing tools that offer sanctuary and assistance to poets at every stage. All a poet needs to do is engage with the idea of community: from sharing work across boundaries and territories, to entering the debates and arguments which give the poetic conversation its vitality. The remedy, it turns out, adds a dimension to the traditional life of the poet: the building of communities where poets can exchange their work and provide a witness to their lives as poets.

– **Eavan Boland**

Alison Hackett

THE LAST TWO POTS OF MARMALADE

The last two pots of marmalade
made by my father,
his handwriting on the lids,
marking the year they were made,
and also the year that he died
2015   2015

I open one and the scent of Seville oranges
conjures him back, here in the kitchen
listening to Radio 4, whistling to himself.
A blast of hot air from the Aga,
the plop of an egg roiling in boiling water,
steaming porridge sprinkled with salt
and sometimes a dollop of cream.
Strong tea, poured from the pot, cup after cup,
slices of toast, edges charred to black,
butter jewelled under a slick of marmalade,
creamy sweetness flecked with citrus tang.

Colette Bryce

HIRE CAR

Later, my iPhone delivers up the name –
Fend Flitzer – this snub-nosed rental calls to mind:
Invalid carrier and direct precursor
of the Messerschmitt, which famously vroomed
on billboards by Saatchi in the late nineties,
around the time you finally quit,
quietly, against all expectations:
too late, Mammy, your lungs already shot.
For decades that was your brand, *Silk Cut*.
What was that advert's message all about?

I can vaguely remember a spike or fin,
as we ease you from the wheelchair, bend
your hinges into the hatchback (memory foam
on the seat for your sore, score brittle bones),
fasten the belt across you with a click.
Not forgetting your tank, 'Jacques Cousteau':
the soundtrack in your house is the slow *whiissht-coo*
of the oxygen in the downstairs bedroom's
constancy, its breathing for you.
These days, the smallest excursion is a win.

Unreachable inside a room / the traffic parts
to let go by, we'll go for a spin as far as Grianan,
stop in at Doherty's on the way back
for a sugared Cappuccino and a Derry bap.
Nozzles in your nostrils, tubes about the ears,
hearing aid: we untangle your glasses.
Handbag, blue badge, paracetamol ...
His hands on the oar / were black with obols.
Are we right? All set? I remember now
what it was about that car. No reverse gear.

Susan Kelly

SUMMER OF '99

Rattling coins in the pocket
of his shiny, mid-grey Farahs,
his left hand clutches a cone
like it's the gear stick of his Massey,
and he attempting Treacy's Hill
with the road sliding beneath the wheels.

Ice-cream melts
down the embossed wafer
and sundae sauce drips
to confuse his busy jumper,
unfashionably festive,
wrong even in the right season.

He leans on the bonnet of his Astra
watching the tide, one foot on the fender
as the engine purrs in the haze.
The Sunday Game crackles from the radio,
county-proud roars drowned out
by interference

and arm-banded children
who split the breeze with squeals
as they bounce on August waves.
Dogs rain on dry-to-the-ankle paddlers
who print the warmed shallows
before moving on.

He bites the hollow tip of the cone
and licks the neon sauce from his fingers,
swallowing fluff from where his fist
rested against his jumper.
The scratchy wool warms
and reddens his neck.

Sated, he clambers into the car
and makes the dial sticky
as he clears the static,
he misses the result and forgets
to check his rear-view mirror
as he backs out from the summer.

Andrew Rahal

ISLAND HOPPING

It's 1885. My future great-great-grandfather renounces the Queen and I am another lapsed All-American.

He leaves Belfast after the trees and potatoes are cleared. He sends money home or he never sends money. I am still weighing the difference.

It's 1978. *Kiss Me, I'm Irish* are the green words on the button my grandmother pins to her lapel in campaign season. It is a working definition.

It's 1995. She uses a fork and knife to cut her napkin. Over the course of dinner, this becomes less and less funny. I learn to redact some memories and accept the oblivion of others.

It's 2020. Our apartment is in a high rise in Finaghy. It is on a to-be-demolished list of buildings. It is the difference between a timer and a clock.

From our balcony, the disappeared oaks and the famine stretch out. It is time they grow together. I am sitting on the couch. My son is in his high chair. The plastic tray separates us.

On a clear day, I can almost see the shipping channel. I can tell him which way the ocean liners are actually heading. I don't have to make it up anymore.

Jonathan C Creasy

GENERATION

> *for Jane Alden*

There is a moment
when the heart stops

silence is the ground,
the sky, the rattling air

made still in new
forms of old notation

Generations fold in
and draw their lines together

Siobhán Campbell

CONSOLATIONS

Jessica Traynor, *The Quick* (Dedalus Press, 2018), €12.50.
John Kelly, *Notions* (Dedalus Press, 2018), €12.50.
Michelle O'Sullivan, *This One High Field* (The Gallery Press, 2018), €11.95.

Something of the sense of life at the nub of it permeates *The Quick*,
Jessica Traynor's second collection. Written with a lightness of touch,
these poems are capable of dealing with the big themes – especially those
of death, birth, and illness. Spare, often short lines, carry their import in
narratives that draw in the reader, sometimes surprising us with similes
that make us think twice: 'her lungs fold like an origami bird'; or, 'the
horizon lifting / / like a cat's third eyelid'.

Some of this work operates with the trusting sense that communicating
moments of shared yearning or loss is the stuff of poetry, and the sense
that an audience is in the picture can sometimes lead to endings that are
slightly less subtle than what has gone before. Where diction becomes
more of interest to this poet, in 'The Witch's Love Song to her Ex' for
example, the sparky dissonance works well within a longer line and
rhythmically assured tercets. And, in 'The Witches Hex an Enemy', there's
a delight in the inherent humour of the hex which leads to memorable
phrasing:

> the unformed id
> of our gestating daughters

That wry humour permeates some of the more ambitious poems too,
where the author seems to move away from the reach for a transformative
moment toward exploring what different forms of the lyric can achieve.
Poems like 'The Artane Boys' Band' and 'Using My Tongue' face the
challenge of writing the public poem, finding a way into the subject matter through form. Occasionally, in the socially-engaged pieces, the satire
might be sharper given this author's wit, as is the case with the multi-
voiced sequence 'A Modest Proposal', but it's with a poem like 'Lord
Haw-Haw' – 'No one has told him he's dead' – that the impulse toward a
sharp, hard-hitting lyric couples well with the ability for striking phrasing:
'he can gossip in the sod / to his raddled heart's content'. This is a satisfy-
ing approach, and shows this poet to be capable of creating canonical
work which draws on a contemporary re-thinking of poetic traditions
while finding a voice that's wholly her own. This is particularly true in
'The Heroes' Chorus', which takes the reader from the Hakka to Tacitus

to Cú Chulainn, and, in a deft move at the end, reveals that its subject may be whether valuing the act of imagination itself may be in jeopardy:

> I let my headset fall, stared at the fields of fallen sheep,
> heard only the breeze, the scurry of leaves.
> The nets of birds, dead from their ordeal,
> we dumped into a ditch.

There's a kind of interruptive, demotic quality to some of the work by John Kelly in *Notions*. The use of inserted speech, in brackets and asides, lends some poems a sense that the speaker of the poem (and possibly by extension, the poet) is wary of being taken seriously, puncturing the wish to be so taken by demurring, like the speaker in 'Goal of the Season': 'Oh, the rhythms of our own self-commentary'. This is, however, compensated for by quieter moments of emotive control, as in 'Winter's Blessing':

> When you bow your head
> to the soloing thrush,
> lit like an old friend's soul
> in the bones of a silver birch.

This work is at its best when naming things with an acute attention, *'Fizzy orange with a straw for me'*, and there's an inviting use of the second person which has the effect of making a pact with the reader, even if the poet is now talking about poetry itself: 'you had to boomerang the word / and hope it glanced precisely'.

In poems like 'Control Zone', visceral memories of the sights and sounds of the Troubles are managed well into poems which imply much more than they say. In another mood, there's an insouciance where the impulse to have fun with words takes off and creates its own dynamic, as in 'Haydn's Skull', where 'a phrenologist found / the musical bump to be very large and very round'. In fact, as one re-reads this work, the title 'Notions' begins to take on extra significance.

There are several narrative poems that tell mini-stories, where the aim of the poet seems to be to capture oddities of lived experience, which he does well, but perhaps in later work he might push up more against his own answers about what the contemporary poem is for. It would be possible to do that and still remain playful of course, and it's that serious play, also befitting the title, that remains the top-note of this book. Most striking is where the impulse for naming meets the wider natural world, often characterised through birds, but also in 'Rats' and 'Pike'. In work like 'Starlings' and 'A Picture of a Bittern', there's a keen ability to render strength of feeling into strong images that are also aurally memorable. It may be that this interest in developing diverse forms of the 'nature' poem is linked to what Forrest Gander says of eco-poetry, that it 'investigates – both thematically and formally – the relationship between nature and culture, language and perception', and it will be interesting to see if forthcoming collections by Kelly expand on these themes.

There's an almost forensic quality to the 'seeing' in Michelle O'Sullivan's *This One High Field*. 'Hijacking the Hare' begins ...

> I turn from field and distant star.
> Cold furs and envelops

... stopping a reader in their tracks with that syntactically demanding use of 'furs' as verb. And now that she's got our attention, we're primed for the rendering of lungs 'filled with nightsong' as 'flight prized to a pocket'. This is work that requires a slow reading and its methods are many, but a favoured one is to move from an inscape of emotional loss back out to the observed world which is now given full metaphoric range. This poem ends:

> This quiet obscure: breath just visible
> and the sudden clear beauty of black
> ice abstracted by strong light.

O'Sullivan has found ways to capture how we actually feel by finding poetic strategies that evoke those feelings. She is not afraid of using apparently awkward phrasing to get close to what is most real: 'An almost there account, a nearly-but-not-nearly-but-not-quite'. This from a poem called 'Cut to an Echo' which, like others, pinpoints moments of relation between people: 'The shadow that made a question of your mouth'. There's a humane sense throughout that this work is in the service of the universal, but it's the exact, sharply apt phrasing and the images which stay in the mind, that make it so successful. A favoured form is that of a fifteen-line poem which has the inward turn of a sonnet, as if five three-line stanzas are the way this poet corkscrews closer to the real import. 'Novice', 'In Convex', 'Endpoint', and 'The Difficult Balance' are fine examples of this not-quite-sonnet and their titles imply a reaching for what she calls 'the difficult balance of the sense of self / that stayed'.

Elsewhere, there's a sense of how people make mind-space in places, an old ice house or an annexe room, and, whether outside at a river or estuary or inside (looking through the many windows that appear in this work), the speaker is often facing up to ambivalence, to the ambiguities of love lost or rejected, or to moments when the human heart is marked, never to be the same again. As O'Sullivan has it, 'like a part-calved ice block threatening a surface', there's passion in this work and it leaks in sure and memorable ways into images of reaching for what will sustain: 'the urge to feel for / the drum of lungwork' ('Abuttals'). And despite the palpable suffering, there are, this work posits, the consolations of being beautifully precise, in an ongoing attempt 'to root at the corresponding somethings', which this book certainly achieves.

Paul McCarrick

PROMISE OF A SUNNY DAY

Galway is the promise of a sunny day with definite certainties of rain
wrapped in another promise of a longer November evening
all trapped in a magician's pocket on Shop Street who promises
you the world but gives you wrong directions to the Claddagh.

Along this trail on this Tuesday afternoon, you see men diving
into big pints of stout, drowsed, defeated, drinking the black stuff.
This plan is their first of many savage plans on the good day.
It is probably their first love; the pints, the defiance, Galway.

You hear them tell this to the women, partners, friends, patrons
with bad timing, now caught in the web of addictive tribal craic.
You see from their full-teeth laughs, their faces shaded with dread
that these pints, with the help of predictive hindsight, will be well-intended.

They love the pint of plain as only they can, but they also love whipped breaths
of wilderness that make the evening, stationary solid stones of coast and walls,
market fresh Saturday mornings. It's what brought you here, organised madness
with enough road markings to fool you to think that, somewhere, there is control.

Galway is probably your first breaking too, the tides high enough to walk across,
the bars low enough to trip over, enough ill-judged nights had to power red
    heaters
for a lashing month in a smoking area for sardines. You are ten-years full of awe
and wonder and have the perfect vision of *cultúr* and can still deny the existence

of a fast-approaching future that blows through these busker-lined paths and
breaks cobblestone cereal bowls. You can look at anyone the way Sally O'Brien
might have looked at you on a Tuesday, but we will remember that today is still
indeed a Tuesday with all the promise of a sunny day and definite certainties of
    rain.

Eoin Rogers

SALLY GAP

Leaving Sunday evening I fix the gate
with the stiff and rusted lock. You watch
from the car, passenger door open, engine running.

Predicting a glut of other weekend travellers
returning to the city you decide the back roads.
You left it late, daylight fading as we leave.

The journey blurs cliff roads into dark
hedged lanes, byways, turnoffs, motorways
until we emerge alone through dark deserted hills.

These roads breathe the curve of slopes
rise and fall running through valleys
open to the moon, where scattered houses glow,

sky and land are tarnished reflections of each other,
dark, silver scrubbed. Headlights flash,
then dim, another car zooms by.

Between us a woman's voice reads cards,
forecasts a stranger's future on the radio.
We move through darkness. You read the road.

Colette Nic Aodha

BEING A POET

'A necklace of wrens': when he was young
Michael Hartnett lay down in a field one day,
Lots of wrens settled on his chest:

Dreoilín, dreoilín, rí na n-éan,
is mór do chuid, is beag tú féin,
éirigh suas, a bhean an tí,
is tabhair dom pingin,
chun é a chur ina luí.

His Granny said that he would be a poet.

I recall laying down on grass at the foot of a hill,
when I was young, out of the sight of my mother,
dodging work.
She told me I was going to be a poet,
but when she spoke
it sounded more like a threat.

Moya Cannon

STARRY, STARRY NIGHT IN THE NATIONAL LIBRARY

Vincent, you would have loved it,
as Don McLean's song poured out
of the bottom, left-hand corner of the reading room
of the Irish National Library,
loudly enough for all twenty-three readers,
drowsy browsers, graduate students,
academics on sabbatical,
to lift and turn startled heads,
like sea-birds grazing a salt-marsh.

He sang for a whole yellow minute, maybe two,
while the readers continued to shift and turn around
not quite upset that their silence had been stolen.
From her curved counter a librarian scanned the desks
and a brown-jacketed, middle-aged man tiptoed
from the catalogue section and gently
closed the lid of a Mac Air, and a long, slow
sigh came from all forty-four cherubs
who had been swinging their plump garlands
high on the green library wall since your time

and I was blown back to a bedsit on South Circular Road
where, forty years ago, I blu-tacked a poster
of your blue and yellow field of stars
at the head of my single bed, not finding it strange
that the stars should swirl like small suns in the pit of night,
not knowing it was painted a year before
you took your own aching, luminous life,
and you, not knowing, as you fought your darkness
and frenziedly harvested the light of stars and sickle moon,
how it would all be poured into a song,
how your brush would flood a library across the sea,
a century later, with golden, starry light.

Virginia Keane

WINTER EVENING

Listening to the fire and sea storm.
I think of my mother old and alone.

I remember at six years old sitting
on her knee wrapped in bath towels

beside this fire, listening to winter storms,
loving my nakedness inside the towel,

singing to ward off bedtime's
separation from fire and knee.

When I'm here alone and dying,
will I be held by fire, by memory?

Rebecca Farmer

SUBMARINE

   1943

My father is sewing
red roses on a white linen cloth.

He waits with thirty men
each breathing in the others' smell.

Some write to sweethearts
letters they might not send,

others sweat and chew
the oil from fingernails.

They long for a cigarette.
Someone listens

for a pulse of sound
from the enemy they can't see.

Fear tastes like metal
on my father's dry tongue,

he can hear his heart beat
as the shadow dives deeper

and from his rough hands
petals unfurl in the stifling heat.

Fred Johnston

BOOKS OF SHARING

Ruth Carr, *Feather and Bone* (Arlen House, 2018), €13.
Michael Coady, *Given Light* (The Gallery Press, 2017), €12.95.
Chris Agee, *Blue Sandbar Moon: a micro-epic* (The Irish Pages Press, 2018), €18 hb.

Some years ago, on my way home from work in a Belfast newspaper, I stepped into a tiny fruit-and-vegetable shop in the centre of Belfast. It was the birthplace of Henry Joy McCracken, and attempts were being made by cultural bodies to have it marked with a plaque; not a great idea then, this was the very height of the 'Troubles', replete with three – or perhaps it was four – British Army turnstile checkpoints along Royal Avenue alone, and the newspaper had already had a bomb threat, neutralised by a disposal robot. There's a Joy's Entry in Belfast, and a super-pub called 'Henry's'. He hasn't been forgotten, one supposes. A United Irishman, he was hanged on the day of his trial in 1798, aged thirty. Beginning as an apprentice organist, the great harp-music collector Edward Bunting lodged with the McCracken family in Belfast for the bones of thirty-five years.

Mary Ann McCracken, Henry's sister, was by all measure an activist; somewhat less so was Dorothy, sister of William Wordsworth, herself a poet and diarist. Mary Ann McCracken was a great support to Bunting and, in her own right, a defender of the poor, chair of the Belfast Charitable Society and leader of the Women's Abolitionary Society at the apex of the slave trade. In her eighties, she was handing out anti-slavery leaflets at Belfast docks. Dorothy Wordsworth shared at least some of McCracken's ideas. Both women were born at the start of the 1770s.

One approaches, then, a collection of poems about two very different women who never met one another, and yet are paired here: why? Different certainly, but in a real sense women of their age, contrasting immensely, products of their social and political environments. McCracken is a woman of social engagement and action; Wordsworth, a quieter recorder of things and people. Unsurprisingly, there are copious historical notes at the back, not always a good thing in a poetry collection, but necessary here. Belfast-born Ruth Carr has done a fine job, let it be said, to line up the two women not in opposition to one another, but almost as complementary sign-posts to the age. Odd, though, that Dorothy Wordsworth is given the greater and the primary space. Her 'voice' permeates the history of herself, which itself appropriates a diary-like feel. There is something injected into Dorothy that occasionally borders on the self-pitying: and just how close was Dorothy to her brother? The critic FW Bateson postulated the darker question many years ago, and it has, by and large, gone unanswered.

Carr, no doubt wisely, doesn't attempt an answer either. Dorothy was accused of unladylike behaviour, say the notes, for undertaking a walking trip with her brother alone. This poem, like many others, is born from a letter. Dorothy elsewhere goes all woe-is-me (William eventually married), and one can't but think that a sojourn with The United Irishmen up on Cave Hill might have stiffened her up a jot: '... while I, / having fought and fretted and striven, / am still seated here by the fire' ('My Dearest Dora'); and, 'how the bells tolled as you lay, / pealing away your life / with the ring of betrothal' ('The Ring').

This is Carr – a tad forcedly – viewing Dorothy and the imagined sense of loss when William married, but is it real? Dorothy got on well with William's wife, and eventually they all lived happily (enough) together. She perhaps veered towards the melancholic anyway. The poem, like all of Carr's poems here, is deftly crafted and startling in its immediacy. But we long for the active engagement of Mary Ann McCracken. And Carr delivers:

> your brother rose to the occasion of his hanging,
> accepted the rope like a garland round his neck.
>
> – 'ON'

And, in 'Kilmainham Letters':

> ... your hand slipping through the bars
> to one who reads in that same light
> beyond the ordered sentence
> of the state, the church, the day
> beyond unequal.

It's not hard to imagine that Carr admires Mary Ann with rather more enthusiasm than Dorothy. She seems more engaged with her, dare one say, more relaxed in her poetry when confronting her. Suddenly the two women are chalk-and-cheese, Mary Ann getting fewer poems but being revealed through what she has as a tougher, earthier, more world-experienced individual, almost approaching the heroic. This is a fascinating and erudite and poetically sound collection; but in the end one feels a Wordsworthian sigh coming on, a 'Poor Dorothy' moment, and one's heart belongs to Mary Ann.

If Ruth Carr makes an attempt to re-jig history in one's perception through twinned retellings of women who had famous brothers (and one might consider the provocative argument that they were two women caught in the shadow of two more historically-relevant male siblings), Michael Coady is a historian of a different kind. Certainly, he is an *archiveur. Given Light* is an archive of things local and intimate in prose, poetry, and photographs, a step forward, arguably, from a collection of poems into the accompanying realms of visual and narrative memory vibrating to the same note; a scrap-book diary, of sorts, in which the close and familiar is given resonance beyond the immediate act of simple recording. The prose pieces have a texture of RTÉ's *Sunday Miscellany* to them; which is to say, they have immediate appeal in a style which is not too taxing yet highly informative. Coady's poetry tends for the most part to eschew imaginative flourishes and flows easily on a current of comprehensible blank verse and prose-lines. In a poem – 'Dear Afterlife' – to the late and much-loved poet Dennis O'Driscoll, the tone is almost conversational:

> And so that's where I'm coming from
> with this on-the-spot
> account of your send-off –
> some details you might wish to scan
> for reference or even just for fun

The poem is flanked by a photo of a round tower and a Virgin Mary staring up at it with hand-wringing intensity – as if some Viking-enterrored monk has locked her out of it – from the vantage-point of a tomb. It is difficult to separate the images from the poems adjacent to them, and one wonders to what degree their positioning is meant to inform the poems, or if they've been placed at random. (Unsurprisingly, one poem is epigraphed with a quote from Henri Cartier-Bresson). A poem such as 'Last Tryst' nudges a stark, lonely, and lovely image – all images are in black-and-white – of a room empty save for a mirror and a chest of drawers and a lightly-scuffed floor of boards. It recalls the poignant images of Walker Evans which illustrated and complemented the great social work by James Agee, *Let Us Now Praise Famous Men*. The poem facing is as lonely as the photo:

> She puts on dark coat
> and gloves, then opens
> the front door
>
> to face
> the morning world,
> the raw east wind ...

'Morning' here conjures up the unwritten word, 'mourning', for this is a poem about a particular type of mourning, a funeral attended by the one-time lover of the deceased who must now process solemnly with the deceased's wife. The simplicity of the poem serves to highlight the emotional intensity of the subject. But the poem and photo fit perfectly, both full of absence, both portraying the unsaid, unstated, the poem and its burden reflecting itself, if you like, in the mirror in the photo. In some ways, the poem is the caption. The question stands: is this placing intentional or accidental?

Coady's urge to record the historic local turns up a translated working of Anthony Raftery's poem, 'Cill Aodáin' (some say the title is more properly 'Cill Liadáin', and blame Douglas Hyde for a mistranslation), a poem familiar to many from schooldays and often sung to the same air as 'The Bould Thady Quill'. 'The Blind Poet's Vision of Spring' is Coady's interpretation of Raftery's waxing nostalgic for Co Mayo; it's beautifully remembered in lines the beat and rhythm of which recall the original Irish and are full of music. He serves up two stanzas here of a poem the original of which ran to at least seven, so we get the basics and the idea. Here again, Coady/Raftery is using the local and remembered to investigate a sense of exile and loneliness:

> I testify here that the heart in me rises
> like a fresh breeze lifting fog from the slopes
> when I think on Carra and Gallen below it,
> on *Sceathach a' Mhíle* or the plains of Mayo.

'A Joyful Haunting' is, for this reviewer, the most fascinating prose piece, a memoir of jazz, of disovering jazz, of the Chris Barber Jazz Band playing in Carrick-On-Suir and of the great Co Down singer, Ottilie Patterson, who married Barber and who died in 2011. I can remember her on the radio from my own teenage days. Coady was 'a schoolboy learner on trombone' when he was introduced to Barber, who advised him to find a good teacher. Coady laments that had 'that option been available to me who knows how it might have changed my life and its direction?' Here is, perhaps, a glimpse of the poet-in-exile from a desired artistic commitment to music; much as many Irish poets are also traditional music exponents or, indeed, part-time painters and photographers. Poetry depends on the seen-and-heard as much as upon any other experience. Are some poets more driven than others to try to encompass in their artistic experience the visual and aural, along with the written? The whole 'holistic' package?

This is a quite remarkable collection of work. It rather goes beyond poetry, though poetry is its main driver. There's great passion underpinning everything here, and a longing, whether it be in Raftery's wish to go back to Mayo, or Coady's musing on a possibly mislaid life as a trombone player. Not a loose note of sentimentality sounds anywhere. Life happens, and one is left with photos, things jotted in margins, and the empty margins themselves. Coady gives light and meaning to a past which is both our own individually and our own in the sense that it is shared. This is a book of sharing. A small gripe: when did Irish poetry publishers cease to print prices on their books? Neither Ruth Carr's nor Michael Coady's collections have prices printed anywhere on their pages or covers.

Chris Agee's founding of the journal, *Irish Pages*, in 2002, marked a significant threshold in Irish writing; the publication continues to occupy an important, not to say central, role in poetry North and South, in Irish – poet Cathal Ó Searcaigh is Irish Language Editor – as well as in English, and provides a well-appointed platform for literary and wider intellectual discussion. The soul-wrenching tragedy of the death of his four-year-old daughter Miriam Aoife in 2001 was framed in Agee's *Next to Nothing* (Salt Publishing, 2009), a collection composed in 2003 and upon which he elucidates: 'In addition to individual poems and several sequences, *Next to Nothing* includes a section entitled "Heartscapes", which consists of 59 "micro-poems", as I call them.' *Blue Sandbar Moon* is also sub-headed as 'A micro-epic', and comprises, save for a few poems by way of lead-in, short bursts of poems that are haiku-sharp, their held emotional energy compressed like some sort of poetical nuclear fusion, and which range over a number of years:

Orange-golden

orb

low over

the Gasworks

in a gap

in the skyline

one carriage

glides in

another

slides out

The poems appear to have been set out with a little extra spacing between the lines, almost an injunction to the reader to take one's time – even if this is accidental, and I don't think it is, the effect is the same. There is no rush, absorb the poem. Let it sink in. The mainly minimalist poems are dated and placed, this one is underwritten as '*Belfast Central Station / 23 May 2010*'. Knowledge of the where and when of a poem obviously locates the poet at the point of composition; further, given Agee's own direction that this collection of 174 poems 'explores ... the emotional and spiritual landscape of a life sustained in the "aftermath of aftermath"', one suspects that they also constitute a mapping of the progress of grief in terms of time and geography, as much as anything else. And one feels that the time-and-location detail is also an intrinsic part of the poem. (He cites in his book-jacketed notes WG Sebald's 'use of photographs in his prose', and his own use of 'a time-signature or imaginative context').

The greater portion of the book comprises a lengthy compendium, 'A micro-epic 2008-2017', where each poem, rather than having a title, has an opening line in a larger type size. Confusingly, a relevant section of the jacket notes which pertain to the present book are in quote marks, which might conceivably convey the impression that they are taken from a review of the book, or a different book altogether. In the Contents – and only there – this long 'sequence' is titled 'Openings', which adds another pinch of confusion. But these are quibbles. The first section, 'Proem', comprises seven pieces of stand-alone poems and some prose. But it's the larger sequence that carries the weight here.

The simplicity of language and bare-bones style of the poems indicate a rawness, a woundedness healing:

The strange thing

is that
Death
is always
the same thing
happening
whenever
it happens.

Žrnovo
8-9 August 2012

There is nothing small, nothing 'micro' about the very human rigours being explicated here, where everything – even a Belfast gas-works – is infused with a sort of stifled cry. Agee's creative victory here is to strip each poem to its nature and, in doing so, invite his readers, whether 'dipping in' to the poems or reading them from cover to cover, to share in the dishevelment of grief and a gradual awakening to the world as it is. Each poem, in that sense, is a meditation or prayer, a key slipped into a lock. One may be reminded of Czesław Miłosz's lines, 'I reached into the heart of metal, the soul of earth and fire, and of water / And the unknown unveiled its face.' Chris Agee has produced a fine and delicately-carved ensemble of important small poems which, taken in their entirety, create a moving and inspiring act of navigation between the seen and unseen, remembrance and experience, sorrow and wonder.

Liz Quirke

WORDS FOR AFTER

When asked how he died, this is all I'll say,
it was on the day before the travels, after all their bags were packed.
A sudden death, fifteenth of June, lunchtime on a Thursday.

I'll tell them all how quick it was, one sharp pain and *that's the way*,
(We heard the phone ringing, but he never called the office back).
When asked how he died, this is all I'll say,

I'm writing out the ambulances, how we thundered night to day,
chasing blue lights over county lines, I'll clear this from the facts,
leave him a sudden passing, fifteenth of June, lunchtime on a Thursday.

I'm cutting out the rushed goodbyes, whispers to stoop and pray,
I'll split the scene and never spill the parts that I can't hack.
When asked how he died, this is all I'll say,

some days (when I can) I'll simply nod and walk away,
I won't relive the ending in retellings back to back,
his sudden death, fifteenth of June, at lunchtime on a Thursday.

I'm giving him an out more kind than the actual run of play,
no Lee view room, no *God is Good*, no terminal decay.
When asked when he died, this is what I'll say, it was:
an easy death, fifteenth of June, at lunchtime on a Thursday.

Rosie Jackson

MY FATHER TRIES TO MAKE AMENDS

All I have left of him is his Bible, in Pitman's shorthand,
its cover black, vanilla-coloured pages leafed with gold.

He was a quiet man, not given to rapture or controversy.
The sound of him riddling the ashes woke me in winter

and how proud he was of me in my school uniform,
or walking me to church twice each Sunday.

'Be good sweet maid and let who will be clever',
urged his copperplate in my autograph book,

and at my shot-gun wedding, he sobbed like a widow.
No one could deliver him then from his black dog

and the next year he opted out of being a father
altogether. Unless you count the help he likes to offer

from the afterlife – when I confess that cleverness
didn't work, and he admits that goodness

didn't do much either. We sit with his heavy Bible
in front of us, his light hand lifting the pages as it did

when I was a child. He reminds me of the 'c'
that means *with*, 'v's that soar like kites' wings,

the simplicity of those mysteries veiled in hieroglyphs –
words like *mercy, tabernacle* – he still loves to decipher.

And I hear the familiar sound of his whisper – *hyssop, lilies,
hearken O daughter, I am poured out like water, my heart is like wax.*

Joanna Klink

LUMINISM

for Mark Strand

It was not important to you that we be
Wrenched awake. You stepped away

From the century into which you were born, turning
Inside, where leaves rained down in wind

And the sea lifted under gusts of white birds.
You were a passenger travelling alone,

Dressed well, making room for acquaintances
And friends, their laughter crossing into yours,

The shadows of their tired bodies, the soft lamps
Of their hands. You saw a world laced with farewells

And held alert the happiness that suddenly
Is here, for a few minutes, among other moods,

Seeming to erase the pull of sorrow. A little
To the side of what was, you kept watch.

Your gracious bearing, the velvet tasks of your voice,
Home after home – the heart in which you slept –

Held no thieving, no grievance, only the far-off music
Of lights and fog. For you, no interior was common.

For you, it was not important to hope. Only to *see*.
To me you extended your hand, saying

The losses are utter, still you might join us,
There is wine in the glass. Mark, dear Mark,

You were more than what we can summon
When we tell stories of you. Your moon

Is the iridium moon that blurs across night,
Your sea the black foam we look for as we ascend.

Your poems rain into our eyes.
We hear you breathe when we dream.

Eva Isherwood-Wallace

EPITHALAMIUM

By ferry on a soft foil sea,
we crossed water
together and laughed
about leaving each other
to drown.

The lough dreamt the monastery
which lies half-remembered
now, in waking,
and I am adjusting
the frame again to capture you
in my coat
and in my shoes.

Every ruin is a wind chime,
and here we are:
our epithalamium
which tastes like a new type of metal
forged from street lights
switching on,
their red lozenges
glowing sickly,
sweet iron.

We stay up all night
god-talking
and saying goodbye to the twenties
we haven't lived yet.
This joy
is pathological.
Tell me,
on which finger would you wear this ring?

Ian Maleney

from 'A KIND OF CLOSING CADENCE'

> *The older you get, in a sense, the more you forget. Vast tracts of your*
> *life sort of vanish in oblivion. But that which survives in your mind*
> *acquires a very considerable degree of density, a very high degree*
> *of specific weight. And of course once you are weighed down with*
> *these kinds of weight, it's not unlikely that they will sink you.*
> — WG Sebald

I went to Seamus Heaney's funeral. His work had meant a lot to me, so
I wanted to mark his passing. I also wanted to see what the funeral of a
national figure was like – I'd never been to something like that before.
Anyway, the church was just a short walk from my flat. I was twenty-two
and unemployed. I had the time to spare.

I got up after Niamh went to work. I showered, shaved, and deliberated
too long over what jacket to wear. I had nothing in black, only a ratty
brown thing that was worn thin at the elbows and coming apart at the
shoulders. I took a photo of myself in the mirror and sent it to Niamh to
get her advice. Walking around nervously that morning, I felt as I always
do before formal occasions – inadequate and under-dressed, an imposter.

It was a warm and blustery day in September. Some lines had
appeared in my head that morning, and I repeated them to myself as I
made my way through the quiet suburbs of south Dublin:

> *I'm going to a funeral,*
> *And you are going to Bellaghy.*

Even though I had never written poetry, I felt inspired by the occasion
and thought that I might work the lines into a poem when the whole
thing was over. I made sure to take special notice of the unusual; the
grown man pushing himself uphill on a child's scooter, the window-
washers hanging off the roof at the Herbert Park Hotel, dark little figures
half a mile up. This is what a poet does, I thought.

I crossed the roundabout outside the church and entered the queue
to get through the side door. There were cameras everywhere. A book of
condolences at the entrance seemed to exert its own kind of gravitational
pull. I scribbled my name for posterity and added *Codladh Sámh*, which I
saw someone else had already written but, feeling no need to be original,
considered ideal for the job at hand. I had nothing of my own to contribute,
in any case.

When I finally got inside the church there was standing-room only
and not much of that. I leaned awkwardly against a wall next to the

entrance to the parish shop. I turned my head to see postcards and religious trinkets on little stands, holy water stacked on shelves like air freshener or shoe-spray. Aware that I was probably blocking the view of someone much more deserving, I slouched down as far as I could. I was able to make out thin tufts of white hair peeking from the tops of cotton white robes on the altar, and an indistinct congregation down the main aisle. The place was lit up like a film set, the solemnity of the event somewhat infiltrated by its spectacle.

—

Heaney always reminded me of John Joe[*], in a way. They were of similar age, and they looked alike. Their lives turned out very differently but they came from the same world of small farmers in out-of-the-way places. Mossbawn felt like home to me, and these parallels helped make the poetry vivid and recognisable. I think sometimes that the only real difference between the two men was education. I see Heaney as someone who learned to question his inheritance, who went away on his scholarship and was never quite able to come back. Though half his siblings emigrated, John Joe lived his whole life in his father's house and never even left the country. But of course it's never so black and white.

For me, Heaney's success was evidence that the kind of inconsequential rural place I knew best could still be worth writing about, and that the touchstones of my parochial upbringing could be made relevant, even telling. It also showed me that my relationship to that place need not be straightforward. Heaney wasn't quite like the family and community he depicted in poems about his early life. He came from them, but he wasn't one of them, not exactly. He was a farmer's first son, but he was a Harvard lecturer too. It was only when he'd moved on that he found his imagination was still rooted in the place where he was born and raised. When writing about that home, he displayed a conflicted self-awareness I immediately understood. In his poems, memories of that place, and those people, are played back like records. Heaney drops the needle on a thin wedge of frozen experience and suddenly it erupts into life on the page.

I thought once that Heaney had negotiated some union in his life, some synthesis of the erudite poet and the hard-working man of the land. It looked as if he'd found a way to balance these different sides of himself, and to live in peace with both. I believe now that I was wrong, and he never did manage this. But I think it was that failure that produced his best work – the most complex, the most ambivalent, the sharpest.

---

* My grandfather, who suffered from Alzheimer's Disease in his final years.

What he left as a child he left forever, and it lived only in memory and verse for the rest of his life, a tug on the string of the mind.

It seems to me that Heaney spent his career responding to that tug on the string. When I'm feeling optimistic, I think it was a way of being thankful for what he'd been given; a way of honouring it, and of keeping it with him. But I think there is guilt there too, and later a wishful escapism. Whatever its motivation, Heaney's writing forms a record of his relationship with home as it changed over the course of his life, an accretion of knowledge, significance and effort – solid and evidential. I can imagine the weight of it, of what one has said and believed to be true. In writing it all down, we give it shape outside of ourselves, and are charged then with carrying it with us always – this separate, uncanny thing that one no longer has the freedom to forget.

—

When I was still in college, Heaney published his final collection, *Human Chain*. My mother bought a copy, which I quickly stole for myself. The poems are quietly concerned with death, and with what it is like to live, for another short while at least, through the passing of one's friends and peers. It was a subject I could sympathise with, having seen Nana and John Joe suffer so many similar losses. My grandparents bore that pain with dark humour, lump-in-throat reminiscence, and the occasional moment of depression. *Human Chain* is woven from the same material – a collection that looks backward, finding what consolation it can in the images and sounds that swim up from the past.

By this time in his life, having survived a stroke and been fitted with a heart monitor, Heaney's memories of childhood were at their most distant and most precious. In 2009, shortly before *Human Chain* was published, Marie Heaney told the writer Robert McCrum that Mossbawn was her husband's paradise. "His Eden," she said. "All he's ever wanted to do is go back." I think those memories of Mossbawn – full of fresh-cut grass and benevolent skies; the taste of picked berries and the touch of insects – are for him an escape both from death's shadow, and from the labour of the writer. They push back against the inevitability of what Heaney called 'a kind of closing cadence' in his life, and they offer an alternative to the writer's duty of bearing witness; of noting down, connecting, drawing out – the responsibility, in the end, of always finding the right words.

The longing to be free of this endless task – or, more depressingly, the eclipse of the task's significance by the prospect of death – gives rise to a pastoral fantasy where language and the natural world are more intimately and unquestioningly sewn together. Words spring, simultaneously and without affectation, from each impression of the world. In *Human Chain*, Heaney is remembering a time where memory itself was not important, where names were given and narrative not yet established. A time or place when all of us were not so busy telling ourselves the stories of our own lives. He's dreaming of an open field while walking in a graveyard. In these final poems, I can feel Heaney yearning for a world where meaning is to be found in the vitality of the experience itself, not in any use that might be made of it. A world where intuition is the limit of understanding, where whatever came, came naturally, and where there is little use for poetry at all because poetry is in everything and not separate from it, like it is for most of us. Living out the end of a life, burdened like a cart-horse by the weight of knowledge and experience – compounded in turn by the suspicion of their futility – I can imagine how this dream of an existence without inheritance, without record, without consequence, might come to seem like paradise.

—

I think the most important word in Heaney's poetry is 'between'. It's there all along, from the first poem to the last collection. Between the moment and the recollection of it, between the experience and the record of it – I think that's where Heaney lived. Neither fully in the present nor wholly in the past, ferried between the shores of each by the leaky craft of memory. The idea implies movement, traversal, and attrition. I think Heaney understood. There is no perfect recollection; you must leave something behind.

To be in-between is to be open to possibility and to change. But it is also to be doubtful, to suspect, to question. How should a poet properly live and write? That was Heaney's question. I ask it with a different inflection: *how can I properly live and write?* Writing divides us from life, in a small but permanent way. We can come close to it again, very close sometimes, but we must always return to whatever shadow of life this is; our life reconstructed from memory, where we carry our truth around with us and display it for others. Writing, for me, means that I cannot live in my father's house. And I cannot leave it either. I must be in-between, ready to preserve what I can, to make use of what I find. When the time comes, will I also long for the escape of imagined childhood, or some other warm oblivion? Heaney on one side, my grandfather on the other. Two paths. I ask as if it were a choice.

'A Kind of Closing Cadence' is the third chapter of *Minor Monuments*, a book of essays by Ian Maleney. Sincere thanks to the author and his publisher, Tramp Press, for permission to include this excerpt.

See **www.tramppress.com**

Lorraine Mariner

LES PARAPLUIES DE CHERBOURG

My uncle lies on the roof
of the youth hostel in Athens
because all the rooms are full.

He cannot sleep. It is not just the heat
or his grief at the death of his father
whose family he has come to find

but the singing, in French,
from the open air cinema;
Catherine Deneuve in a raincoat

her heart breaking, night after night,
But I'll never be able to live
without you ... Don't go. I will die.

It is 1964. My uncle is 21.
No need to sleep, dear uncle,
hum along, count the stars.

There is separation and rain
and a remembrance. I open it again
like an umbrella.

Grace Smith

SESTINA FOR RED SHOES

My mother sometimes gardened in red shoes
she would just have forgotten to change them
no help I would stay inside to just watch
our garden had grown into a suburban wild
laughing off all my mothers hard work
on it grew greeny dense and dark

In a burst she would garden well into dark
and then come in with mud caked shoes
I couldnt see the point of this hard work
cutting things and soon again cutting them
the garden had a notion to grow wild
better to stay inside and just watch

Women stand at the windows and watch
smoking through night flames in the dark
it was wrong to let your garden grow wild
they thought and then frowned at her shoes
we always seemed to be different to them
and fitting in seemed such endless hard work

My mother went daily to an office for work
drove off as others stayed home on watch
hair flying belt missing prettier than them
untidy glamour long legged and dark
smirking they glanced at her shiny red shoes
but a widow cant be seen to be wild

Its dangerous to be thought of as wild
enough to be different as a widow at work
and to stride the town in shiny red shoes
knowing how the others do like to watch
just stay inside with your child in the dark
its best to avoid notice say them

The small world of us two many more of them
vesta beef curries and a garden growing wild
old pictures of my mother laughing full dark
hair now greying and pinned up at work
like the others I stand back and watch
learning to frown at the sight of red shoes

Pleasing them can be a lifetimes work
and the wild brings the weight of the watch
let the dark be lit by a pair of red shoes

CL O'Dell

SUN MOTH

Last night came back in the afternoon,
with wings –
            evidence
we had forgotten
a part of us there.
                    Stars smudged on our lips
and the moon,
            buried somewhere
in the sky, lost
            inside our mouths.

My hands
were unable to write it all down
in a dream,
I remember,
            not a single shadow
was ignored. Passing cars turned to waves
and crashed on the front lawn.

The part of us I needed
                    burned
and in the ashes I found my body again
at the beginning, with no evidence
of ever being so
            alive.

Laura Potts

SWANSEA SON

He is here in my autumn of age
the riverlight through windowpanes,
the small-hour laughter,
the slim-supple night,
and moonlight eyes on the history page.

I remember his name that giggled the stars
when the stage of the world lit its lights for him,
and I, summer's daughter,
he Swansea's son
whose words in the plash of the water
we hear in the echoes of hills. Still

the ghost in my arms in the cracked black night,
still in stairwells that old grey light that writes
of the deer shaping the dales, that writes
of bonfire-bright half-pint ale, that writes
of Death in His coat and tails:

you, man of words with the firefly eyes,
who didn't stay to see the wild spring flowers
riot on the mountainside, who died
like a steeple that cradles its bones,
and whose voice now sleeps beneath Wales' stones,

you, my lone man with the light, lord of all words,
whether I'm there with you or not, well, that's alright.

Jaki McCarrick

HOME AND AWAY

Jo Burns, *White Horses* (Turas Press, 2018), €12.
Rachel Coventry, *Afternoon Drinking in The Jolly Butchers* (Salmon Poetry, 2018), €12.
Rachel McCrum, *The First Blast to Awaken Women Degenerate* (Stewed Rhubarb Press, 2018), £10.99.

The three writers whose debut collections are reviewed here share some background, a commonality which shows up in their poetry. Jo Burns and Rachel McCrum hail from Northern Ireland, and both seem to have left at a young age. Subject matter such as Ulster, the sea, home life, appears in the debut collections of both poets, who now live abroad, McCrum in Canada (after years in Scotland), and Burns in Germany (having travelled the globe). Rachel Coventry was born in Scotland, and after ten years in London is now resident in Galway. Hence, these are women who have all experienced exile and emigration. Also, the subject of their gender and of contemporary (and historical) feminism is present in all three works.

Burns's *White Horses* is divided into four sections, 'Eclipse', 'Oceans', 'Gravity', and 'Revelations'. Each of these explores specific themes and points in the poet's own life, with some overlaps from section to section. There are also numerous references throughout the collection to horses. 'Eclipse' primarily explores the life, loves, and work of Pablo Picasso. My favourite of the poems here is 'Guernica', in which Burns gives voice to various characters in Picasso's eponymous painting. Like much of the work in this section, 'Guernica' is full of short dramatic lines such as 'War covered the sun', and 'They came on market day'. The enigmatic presence of the white horse in Picasso's painting is beautifully described: 'Paint can't hold his aura, spirit as white pulse streams into shore, spindrifting.'

In 'Oceans', Burns returns to the Northern Ireland of her childhood and, occasionally, to the Rhodesian roots of her grandfather. Often written in couplets, the poems here cast a cold, sometimes suspicious eye on her past. A favourite here is 'Paperweight from Home', in which a glass paperweight that stands 'on bills, school letters, / unticked to-dos' contorts the images it reflects, offering those who pick it up new ways to view the world. The final poem in this section, 'Felice Bauer's Last Letter to Kafka', is also particularly affecting. Here, two lovers watch a pair of ravens and see in the birds' behaviour their own dynamic: 'When I'm building nests for us both in my mind, / you crave the swoop, the throng and the flight.' It's a subtle reflection on a marriage, and segues seamlessly into the next section, 'Gravity', which is the most personal section in the book, and its most powerful.

In the opening poem here, fittingly entitled 'Conception', the speaker, travelling in Chile, is amazed to discover she's pregnant: 'A woman, / scared of babies. A globetrotter, / shocked'. The excitement of travelling is compromised suddenly by the constraints – and wonder – of pregnancy: 'It's night. I cannot fight it all', she opines. That's a powerful line in which the reader registers immediately the overwhelming confusion this unexpected news has brought. This is followed by one of the strongest poems in the entire collection, 'Phaethon'. Now the previously anticipated baby is a teenager, diagnosed with an illness. In this poem the image of the speaker's son, 'paled, in the Helios hospital', having been struck ill after a week in which he painted his own bedroom, is conflated with the myth of young Phaethon, riding his chariot (again those horses) across the sky and quickly losing control, his young life as 'mortal white bones ablaze'. 'On Faith' comes aptly after this, with the poet questioning her relationship with faith, something she thought she'd left behind in Ireland:

> I've seen enough indoctrination to make long lists
>
> and formed my own image of you to suit my nature,
> closed your book to open others only to discover words
>
> that I needed and looked for were already under my tongue.

The final section, 'Revelations', contains a number of political poems. I enjoyed this section immensely. 'Heart or Reason' charts contemporary life in Germany, where Burns has lived for a number of years. In an obvious reference to Brexit and the current wave of nationalism/populism in the UK, its speaker insightfully declares: 'It's our duty to warn how nations are duped when uncertain. / We have been there but now it's looking red, white and blue.' Many of the poems here examine the recent well-publicised arrival of refugees and asylum seekers to Germany. In 'Christmas Shelter', the story of Fata Morgana, an asylum seeker now living in his *Unterkunft*, whose family he left behind in an unnamed country, is conflated with the story of Joseph and Mary. Exile and emigration are examined again in 'Exodus', in which Angela Merkel's much publicised assertion '*Wir Schaffen das*' is seen as a slither of hope to the stateless, who lament that 'a land can be / an old crocodile, / letting you call it home, then spit you out'. In 'Piano (after the Forte)' there is much appreciation of the work done in the latter days of the Peace Process by Martin McGuiness: 'we've the right to be judged / by our last *fermata* and *al fine* note'. Ever-present in Burns's remarkable debut is an Ulster upbringing, never forgotten, informing travels across the globe and to the tops of mountains ('Green Milk'), as well as domestic life in Germany.

Galway-based poet Rachel Coventry was born in Edinburgh to an Irish mother and Scottish father and, as mentioned, has lived for a decade in London. All these components of her background make an appearance in her gorgeous debut, *Afternoon Drinking in The Jolly Butchers*. I adored this distilled and spiky work. Coventry's collection is divided into three sections which chart a timeline from the past to the recent past to the present. A number of poems in Section One explore drug use, such as 'The Lost', in which the speaker watches a friend shoot up: 'I said nothing in protest though / I could not watch the needle go in', and 'Poppies', in which a long-ago holiday in France is remembered, possibly with the same friend referred to in 'The Lost':

> We fed on waxy balls of
> opium. I cannot say how long we stayed but one night the moon
> was more full and more beautiful than it has ever been since.

This compellingly dark relationship is explored again in 'Multiverse', in which the speaker imagines alternative worlds for herself, one where 'you get clean, read physics, a mature student / at Leicester University'; and where 'I leave London / before it's too late'. In these first poems the lines possess a sense of personal unburdening with which the reader instantly connects. There's some longing for London, too, as in 'Beat':

> I am still haunting the old addresses
> oblivious to cosmetic improvements,
> wandering pre-gentrified Stoke Newington
> lost in a maze of grey council estates

Section Three brings us bang up to date, with many of the poems set in Ireland (Galway mostly), where Coventry is now based. These explore the (supposedly) uneventful everyday: walking the dog, observing birds, waiting in bus stations, time spent in the company of an elderly mother, moments with lovers. Coventry has a striking ability to mine the achingly bleak for cracking lines: 'If we could be transformed into otters / would you slip with me into black water' (from one of three poems titled 'I have feelings for you'). In the Larkinesque 'Adult Single', the loneliness of the speaker is personified as a man: 'I cannot stand his weak limbs / his painful lack of confidence // I have resisted him an age / but he never gives in'. 'November 2016' features a murmuration of crows (rather than starlings) which has 'dispensed with the song, / the jolly chattering, the whistle and chime / they filled up the air with'. This is a fantastic poem, and the choice of the quotidian crow over the lyrical starling is typical of Coventry's deliciously irreverent style.

Rachel McCrum's debut has an enigmatic title, *The First Blast to Awaken Women Degenerate*. An ambitious collection, it largely explores the lives and roles of women in contemporary society, in McCrum's native Northern Ireland and in Scotland, where – until recently – she was BBC Scotland Poet in Residence. There are also poems here about the world's climate crisis, and thus the collection as a whole feels strikingly current, turbo-charged by McCrum's whip-smart voice. The opening poems explore growing up in Northern Ireland, always with an emphasis on female characters or female-centric narratives. In 'Broad', the speaker says, 'My mother was a farmer's daughter with a voice / that stretched across three fields.' The poem refers to a mother who stresses that 'it is important to get the potatoes // on the table for your brothers / before you write the application / for the university'. This, we learn, is a woman who herself had been to university, who 'did both', but who nonetheless 'grew, along the way, uncharacteristically quiet'. Here the pragmatism of the speaker's family is at odds with her plans for herself – and in the last stanza she invokes Heaney's 'Digging': 'I have only one callous to show them. / The indentation between the knuckles / of the middle finger of my right hand.'

'I Go Sailing' is a heartfelt account of the speaker's experience at the helm of a boat in which she and her father have sailed out to sea. The boat gets into trouble and her sailing skills are tested in 'A heightening gale, / the pitch and maw of big water.' In 'Do not Alight Here Again', Northern Irish parents, themselves accustomed to emigration, urge their children to 'Exile yourselves', and 'Be better than us.' 'I am Gigi Hadid's Left Elbow' is a powerful series of quatrains in which the speaker claims the various body parts and qualities of iconic women. I loved in particular the lines, 'I am Gina Miller's balls', and 'I am Susan Ballion's pseudonym'.

McCrum's championing of women continues with the title poem, 'The First Blast to Awaken Women Degenerate', which counters John Knox's polemical work, *The First Blast of the Trumpet Against the Monstruous Regiment of Women* (1558), in which Knox lambasts female monarchs, arguing that female rule is contrary to God's will (Elizabeth I detested Knox). McCrum's poem is a clever riposte to this. In it she imagines the very women who might emerge after Knox's 'trumpet' sounds: 'seismic cunt women / bloody pushy women', and 'Women who sink a bottle of red / and rage with wine lips women'. It's a real thrill to see such a controversial medieval text given a long-overdue shakedown. This is followed by 'Oh My Fathers', in which the men of Ulster are admonished for doing little to help the plight of women who, after 'the mills / had already been shut', lost a great deal of independence. 'Where did you leave your women?' the poet asks, replying, 'In the kitchens, at the sinks, / paring down, paring down / to the red sore quick of their nails.'

These are fantastic debuts, each deserving of prizes and the utmost praise.

Paddy Bushe

AMERGIN'S SHIP

for Holger Lönze

Because he wanted simply to be as one
With the swelling wave and the wind,

With the salmon and with the stars
Clustered in the eye of the gannet,

He sailed north when the four winds
Blossomed together in a compass,

North being the petal that trembled
Towards the grey ambiguous headlands

The elder swore he scried from the tower
Infinitely far beyond the salty horizon.

The ship's skin-lined planking breathed
Brine and wind, welded gust and swell

In a coupling that surpassed navigation.
Sea and ship hammered one another

Into one another's shape, shaped
Wind and weather to the poet's will

To be the voyage, to be the landfall
And the words that marked the landfall,

To be the land and the land's creatures
To be the stones raised in commemoration,

To be the ship beached forever on the land,
And the words singing themselves into bronze.

Larry Stapleton

CARROWMORE

> *passage tombs were being erected there ... several*
> *centuries before the large Boyne Valley tombs*
> — Bergh and Hensey, 2013

Only now do we know this land
on either side of a quiet lane
on the outskirts of our town
was where a country began,
a people first made a mark,
no longer hunter-gatherers
but farmers – and builders
of this wide necropolis,

of the tombs we can see
on so many distant hills,
the great cairn of Knocknarea –
high now on the skyline
as we follow the grassy trail
leading to Listoghil, the cairn
at the heart of Carrowmore.

All around us, boulder circles
and dolmens, passage tombs
of a people who wore rings
made of sperm whale teeth
or walrus ivory, and fastened
their garments with pins
of bone or red deer antler –
mushroom-like pinheads
on fragments found
in the burial chambers;

and perhaps like that, still,
if we listen, from Listoghil,
or somewhere in the ring of hills,
we may one day pick up an echo,
come to hear a silence sing.

Joe Carrick-Varty

A WEEK AND NOT A WORD SINCE THE ARGUMENT

I'm cycling near your house,
cycling for no reason, to nowhere,
but I'm near your house, on your road in fact,
passing the Baptist Church
and the redbrick half-finished new build
and in no time at all the shape of you is walking towards me
slap bang in the middle of the road.
We talk, albeit gingerly, about my work at the playscheme,
about the kids who fight there,
about my sister off to Uni in a month –
to Glasgow! As if she could've picked a further place.
You slur only a little when you say that.
Where you off anyway?
Nowhere.

The barman you call Mason nods,
unlocks the side door, props it open,
motions you inside. I look at my watch: 11 a.m. –
I'm seven years old, waiting with a Coke outside
the frosted glass of The Seven Stars,
smelling cigarettes every time the door bangs –
then I'm you, in Coventry, your father
at the bar, more hair than the both of us, taller
in the backlit glow of the doorway
than I'd known him from the black and white photo
you stuck to the fridge one Christmas Eve.
You gather us around, whiskey-whisper *this is your Grandad,*
no liver cirrhosis, not dead at 48,
still bringing pork scratchings and a bottle of fizzy pop
to land with a clink on the step.

So, you coming in or not?

Regan Good

THE DUDDO STONES: STONE CIRCLE IN NORTHUMBERLAND, ENGLAND

Cutting through the barley by permission, we
approached for fifteen minutes, our hands barely
touching the barley tips, like a reluctant mother
touching the head of her child, or a swarm of children.
Come, follow me, nascent babies of the barleycorn,
your father has been sacrificed by the sickle and is gone.
His blood was spilt so you could thrive and grow;
his blood nourishes the bulbs and every sucking straw.
He died as you will die, but he died savagely
so that you could live in harmony – human blood spurt
from his stem strengthened your receptors to the sun.
Some sheaves, bright green and hard, arch over others,
baring fuzzy whiskers like a New England caterpillar.
The barley near the creek was yellowed as wet wheat,
waterlogged and rotten and therefore no good for bread.
We walked like gladiators through the triumphal path
to the stones.   It was the pathos of the approach,
through food we could not eat, seed-shells, hard roots,
some yellow, some stained, hard glums and peduncles.
The lustreless world was made lustreful by wind
rustling through potentialities, seeding something else.
When we reached the stones, the world went dim.
The barley babies darkened and rushed at us frantically
as if we were abandoning them. No, no, I said. I am
the end. I am of the Duddo stones. I am a charnel spot.
I am not your mother; I cannot soothe you in my arms.
Changed by rain and wind, like in the Shakespeare song,
channelled and scored, so changed we both resemble
oyster shells or giant cat paws erupting from the hill.
You are alone, you have no mother, as I have no brother.
We walked back through the yellow babies hungering,
wishing for the bloody sickle to cut and feed the field.
The Barley Mother was a dry husk we carried home,
and hung over the breezeway door. Look, here she is,
drying out, and in black wet spots, she's mouldering.

Pádraig Ó Tuama

ENJOY YOUR PINT

At the bar,
in an unknown part of Birmingham
I bought two pints
and paid with paper money
from the northern part of Ireland.

That's not British money,
the publican said.
And I said, yes it is,
you'll see the royal head
if you hold it to the light.

And a man standing right beside me
turned to me and looked and said
So you're from Northern Ireland.
He was wearing
denim jeans and a denim jacket,

tobacco fingers fixed round a half-drunk pint.
He locked his eyes on me and
moved so near I could have kissed him,
Whose side are you on, son? he whispered
Whose side are you on?

And I didn't know the landscape of belonging
in this part of England.
I hadn't seen signs enough to know
whether his hope flew for
the orange or the green.

He continued to look.
He continued to keep close.
And I said
I hope for
peace.

And he said
That's a clever answer,
son.
That's a very
clever answer.

And I said
I know.
Enjoy your pint.
And I
got up to go.

Matthew Geden

THE BACKWARD STEP

Fred Johnston, *Rogue States* (Salmon Poetry, 2018), €12.
John Liddy, *Madrid and Other Poems* (Revival Press, 2018), €12.
Dawn Wood, *As Mind Imagines World* (Templar Poetry, 2018), €12.
Susan Lindsay, *Milling the Air* (Doire Press, 2018), €12.

The term 'rogue state', as the blurb on the back cover of Fred Johnston's
Rogue States points out, is generally used to describe countries that have
fallen out of favour with the West, in particular with the USA, and
thereby present an apparent threat to the stability of key regions of the
world. Here, however, the term also encompasses the poet's own physical
wellbeing as the rogue state of serious illness threatens his very existence.
Johnston sees himself at risk as he joins the 'waiting-room brigade', as
cancer redraws 'the borders we knew by heart'. As the collection
progresses, it becomes more and more evident that the sickness inside is
mirrored by perceived social and political problems in the wider world.
    The opening poem, 'Cancer Unit', is a fine example of the understated
tension which lies just beneath the surface of this book. Each tercet has a
regular rhyme, giving a sense of unity nicely at odds with the 'gruff fidgety
anticipation' and 'the train-clack fret / *Not yet, not yet, not yet*' at the close
of the poem. The rhyming words in the fourth stanza highlight the
progression of fear felt by those in this limbo, as the words move from
'error' to 'help her' to 'terror'. There is a sense of powerlessness here as
those waiting feel an absurd thrill when the nurse enters and, 'Names are
sweetly called, but not you, not yet'.
    The poem 'Surgical Strike' is darkly humorous, as the poet compares
the 'rooting out' of his cancer to the United States bombardment of the
caves of Tora Bora in eastern Afghanistan during December 2001. The
fatalistic tone of the poem is reflected elsewhere, and the lack of self-
pity is admirable. In 'Diagnosis', for instance, Johnston notes how swiftly
one's world can change: 'you went in one man and emerge / as another'.
These shifts in identity occur in other poems, and in particular in tandem
with the ageing process – in 'Golden Age' the writer reflects on the ugli-
ness of youthful behaviour, and now, at an age when 'it's an effort to
make / / a cup of tea', he looks back with regrets.
    Johnston is a skilled poet, able to flow between poetic forms and to
cover the personal and the political in a calm, unshowy manner. The
darkness hinted at in the title of this collection comes through in later
poems, such as 'Now That The War Is Over' and 'A Poem For You', the
latter written after the visit of a dance group from a refugee camp in Pal-
estine. In this collection, Johnston, in the face of illness, casts a cold eye

on the world around him, still able to admit, 'We get it wrong about one another / right up to the end'.

John Liddy is also a long-established presence on the Irish literary scene, and *Madrid and Other Poems* is his eleventh book. Liddy was born in Cork but brought up in Limerick, and for a poet where place is a significant inspiration, it is the latter city, along with the Madrid of his present home, which takes precedence in his work. His first book, *Boundaries*, came out in 1974 when Liddy was only twenty and, like his fellow Limerick poet Desmond O'Grady, his talent was nurtured in that city even when he headed out into the wide world. Since then he has worked as a teacher and librarian in Spain, and has continued writing his own work and translating the poems of others.

This new collection is divided into three parts, and each part is arranged alphabetically by poem title in, as a note clarifies, a tribute to librarians and libraries. Indeed, the notion of tribute looms large in the book as a whole, as Liddy pays his respects to poets, artists, and friends as well as to the places he has lived in. The first section, 'Praise', opens with memories of Benedict Kiely, whose influence and genius spreads 'by his presence and his books'. A poem or two later and the reader is in Madrid looking through the eyes of the Spanish poet Ángel González, whose own childhood in Asturias lingers like Liddy's Limerick even in the streets of the Spanish capital. This is one of the strengths of the book, the way the alphabetisation of titles brings about a more random arrangement, allowing for the element of chance discoveries within poetic juxtapositions.

The second section, 'Tort', attempts to broaden the book's scope by bringing in social injustice, political hypocrisy, and the ongoing refugee crises. Whilst some of the poems are strident, there is also an acknowledgement of the fact that social media platforms can create a tired cynicism, where truth has been subsumed by opinion:

> in these cyber
> chattering times amongst the twitt-
> ering classes, where news is fake
> and fact conveniently incomplete

Musings on Brexit are soon replaced in the final section by a return to the familiar territory of Limerick and Madrid, the places that bind the book together. Naturally, thoughts of Ireland produce a nostalgia for a different, more eccentric time, as evidenced in 'All Out': 'But I miss the drama queens on both sides, / the resident oddballs, the gay old times'. The long poem 'Madrid' also takes in the past, but manages to intertwine both personal history and a potted history of the city itself. It is, like many of the strongest poems here, largely concerned with place and belonging, as Liddy is grateful for 'A life gifted to me here, lived amongst you'.

Dawn Wood is another poet who has travelled widely. She was born in Omagh, Co Tyrone, but now lives in Scotland, having also spent time in Andalusia and, more recently, in New Zealand. She is also an artist, and visual imagery in *As Mind Imagines World* is very much to the fore. The poems here draw the reader in to a personalised imagined world which often changes perspective suddenly, and at times gives the writing a hallucinatory quality. Wood has published six collections of poetry, four of which, including this one, were brought out by Templar Poetry in England. The first of these, *Quarry*, was shortlisted for the Aldeburgh First Collection Prize in 2008. She has a background in science and trained as a microbiologist at Queen's University, Belfast, and is also a hypnotherapist whose practice involves exploring the healing power of words and the realms of the subconscious mind.

This multidisciplinary approach gives the poems their main power, a shifting ambiguity reflecting perhaps the way the mind assimilates so much varied information as a person travels through the world. The opening poem, 'Epiphany', sets the scene, positioning the collection in the mind of the reader: 'Imagine a village square', she begins. Within the first few stanzas the poem flits through references to Christmas, the snowman from the film *Frozen*, the EuroMillions, Einstein, Mother Teresa, and Jesus. It is a bewildering progression, where even 'the watchmen / you'd ask would be geckos', but it works as a sort of loosening up of the imagination for the work that follows.

A poem such as 'Strong Man Juggles Sledgehammer and Fire' illustrates the way in which the modern world is in rapid flux. Here 'not even the headlines on the Zurich Tower linger', and the news is interrupted by the sound of a busker who, in turn, is interrupted by 'mothers, children, pigeons', and the poet achieves a temporary stillness as she watches, even though:

> The words were circling round my brain
> but I couldn't quite grab them

Whilst such poems reflect the nature of contemporary society and the human mind, others seem envious of nature itself, which has a freedom lacking in the man-made world. The poem 'Flocklones', for example, expresses a yearning for a place where long-tailed tits might appear as 'a tumbling cohort of arrival to flit between the branches of free flight'. In 'Waves at Manly Beach', the sea draws the poet back to a dreamlike memory of childhood where 'your room is never where you thought', but ultimately the poem embraces the natural world and the remembered father:

> and you do as Daddy taught you –
> you wade out and you swim in.

Susan Lindsay has worked as a psychotherapist, consultant, and trainer for many years before retiring in 2012. *Milling the Air* is her third book from the redoubtable Doire Press. She is also a founding editor of *Skylight 47*, as well as an experienced workshop facilitator. Aside from her previous collections, she has published poems in several journals and anthologies, and has developed a distinctive and original voice. Lindsay's writing is at times wry and humorous, but it has a serious intent, and the rapid changes in our world also figure in her poetry. Her lightness of touch can be seen in her use of free verse, but the poems are well-crafted and contain some interesting internal rhythms and rhymes.

Early on in the collection, climate change and our impact on the environment seep into the poems. In 'Dive-Bombing Dragonfly' the insects remind the poet of the disturbance of wind farms, whilst in the Roger McGough-inspired 'Shall we get swept away by lunchtime', a walk along a pier is a risk, 'Thisbeing a time / of climatechange ... and riverbanksupheld'. Another poem, 'Recycling Planet Earth. Live Art.', details clambering over piles of rubbish 'just to get in the front door'. This latter poem also shows how quickly the world changes, as 'former treasures' soon become mere 'trash'.

In fact, like the previous three poets, Lindsay is interested in the flux of modern society, as she realises that one cannot simply return to the past so one has no choice but to accept the way things are now. In 'Old Ways Confuse' she writes:

> I discover that only by disregarding
> once valuable knowledge
> of the old ways
> can I find my way now.

This seems to go against the grain, but is, for her, part of a 'constant reimagining requisite / to navigating life today'. The poem 'Ireland 2030', on the other hand, looks forward to a strange new world with driverless cars, robots in the fields, and 'smart-phones on the wrist'. Clearly, we are not far from this scenario and in Lindsay's view such innovations may allow us more social time, 'now there's no need / to drive'. *Milling the Air* is a collection which, as the title implies, combines the technological world with the natural one. Human development or 'progress' goes on regardless, but poets such as Lindsay are there to take stock, to point out the changes, to record them and provide a timely reminder, and to 'step back, meditate' as she writes in 'O Maturity, Maturity'.

All four of these poets step back from the world just enough to document how quickly it all moves on.

Nidhi Zak/Aria Eipe

BE/CAUSE

because nothing is like anything
            else, an approximation will always break
                        down when you need it most

because nothing is as soft as a horse's muzzle
            at the curve, above quiet punctuations of hair,
                        thin pointed teeth guarding tenderness

because I had just been, that morning,
            at my college graduation – *looking gorgeous*
                        in that dress – where the speaker urged:

I hope you will be vulnerable
            with each other, that you will be open
                        to giving and receiving vulnerability

because he touched me without asking
            saying: *you are like nothing*
                        I have ever seen before

like how I am touching this horse
            feeling its likenothingelse before, us
                        two silken manes, two hurt mouths

I am so gentle with you between my hands
            but tell me / strike my face / pull away
                        do you not want me to

blow slow into the open black
            tunnel of flared nostril, wet
                        dark animal breathing back

that's how they kiss – a passing
            stablehand spoke in my direction –
                        and I believed him

                                                I believed him
                                    not / because it was true
                                    but / because I wanted to

Deborah Bacharach

LOT'S WIFE, WAITING

The war of kings
was lost. Those left
fell into tar.
She'd been captured
before.

At the camp for
displaced persons, she
waited for the Red
Cross packets of
unleavened bread,
for the child soldiers
leaning on their AK-47's,
twirling them
like white booted
majorettes
in a corn country
parade, to grow bored
and fire.

She drew her name
in the stomped ground.
It's probably
still there.

Patrick O'Donnell

ANNIE

She swirls the water
in the bottom of the enamel bucket
before spilling it onto the dry stones
watching it dampen them.
Another birthday, fifty-seven years
gone by, she measured her lot,
it didn't take long.
She hadn't the money to emigrate
and no man asked for her hand,
the highlights, mass on Sundays
and a neighbour calling.
She thought of John, the way he smiled
she knew he liked her,
but he wasn't forward enough to ask.
She turns back into the cottage
it's time to get the dinner ready,
her two bachelor brothers
would soon be back with their
moods and grunts eager to be fed.

Camilla Lambert

THE SEA HAS MANY VOICES

The whale had been rolled in two days before,
hidden by sea fog. Now it stank of fatty rot.
Spray blew over, sharp and salty on my lips
as I grabbed the warmth of my father's hand,

as we passed oystercatchers in the surf,
a military mob piping in haphazard time.
In that summer of empty cisterns, spent wells,
cooling sea voices brought relief for thirst,

but this whale would no more send its song
of clicks and creaks to sound between the islands.
In slipping light its white skin was dulled,
its bloated body more awkward, less ghostly.

A foghorn boomed, its sobs circling the bay.
They left me untouched; the creature had lived
too hugely, too exotically for a child to grieve.
I turned from its marooned bulk and ran,

leaping across the sand to be alive, my feet
too quick for jab of scattered razor clams.
On the path back up the cliff, teasel heads
scraped my bare arms with whisper music.

Charlie Bondhus

FAMILY VALUE

My brother used his .243 Weatherby Vanguard
Youth hunting rifle to kill white-

tailed deer in the forest around our house.
He'd take me with him sometimes and we'd lie

flat as flapjacks beneath the leaves until
a deer came, and then, crack crack,

I got to understanding death's smooth and black,
sometimes cold, sometimes hot,

but something we control, like what
to plant, or which preserves

we make into pie.
When the ice melted on the lake we'd paddle

across its flat, dark surface, pretending
we were passing through a gun barrel.

My brother would tell me stuff
only older boys are supposed to know – like how

to make a temporary pussy out of rubber
bands and hot dryer sheets or

how keys can be brass knuckles in a pinch.

I never told anyone
I was the first to find Dad

in the snow with a hole
in the back of his head

and his Remington resting
on his chest. His bare toe was curled

around the trigger. The only other
thing I remember that day

was seeing a fat spider in the mulberry bush
and crushing it with a rock.

Laoighseach Ní Choistealbha

EARTH AND WATER

Ceaití Ní Bheildiúin, *Agallamh sa Cheo: Cnoc Bhréanainn: 52.2352 °T, 10.2544 °I* (Coiscéim, 2019), €10.
Doireann Ní Ghríofa, *Lies* (Dedalus Press, 2018), €12.50.

Upon opening *Agallamh sa Cheo: Cnoc Bhréanainn 52.2352 °T, 10.2544 °I*, by Ceaití Ní Bheildiúin, the reader is plunged into a distinctive landscape: the landscape of Cnoc Bhréanainn (Mount Brandon), located on the Corca Dhuibhne peninsula in the Kerry Gaeltacht. I appreciated the geographical coordinates that are given with the title; it assisted in reminding the reader of the physical, looming presence of the mountain in a collection that attends mostly to its otherworldly aspects. The structure of the work is certainly notable. The reader is guided carefully through the collection, which is divided into titled sub-sections, each title giving a hint as to the topic of the poems therein: 'Agallamh leis an gCnoc', 'Na Dreapadóirí', 'Nás Báis', 'Am Dath Cnoc Ceo', 'Fothain', 'Iníon an Chnoic', 'Treoir go Parthas', and 'Aisling'.

This work is all the more distinctive due to the inclusion of different personae that speak to us throughout the poems: An Cnoc, Deisceabal an Chnoic, Dreapadóirí an Chnoic, Taibhse Chogaidh, Taibhse, Iníon an Chnoic, Áitritheoirí, Cuairteoirí, Abhainn, and Scál. Even though this collection focuses on Cnoc Bhréanainn as a kind of geographical and spiritual muse, the differing personae contribute greatly to the variety of the poems, which include pieces relating to folklore and tradition ('Chomh Mear le Mis', 'An Lucht Sí is an Teilifís'), emigration issues and returning emigrants ('An Poncánach', 'Tigh Ar Ceant'), family bereavement ('Taisí'), as well as present-day disasters in the Middle East ('Tar agus Tóg').

Rooting all of these topics in the omniscient presence of Cnoc Bhréanainn is achievement indeed. The high point of this variety is found, in my opinion, in the section 'Nás Báis' in the middle of the book; this section presents us with the events of history from the experience of the mountain itself, who appears to be haunted by 'Taibhse Chogaidh' and 'Taibhse', two of the aforementioned personae who take centre stage in this section. These voices speak of various historical events, including the Great Hunger, the Easter Rising, 1916, the Irish Civil War, and the coming of Lord Grey to Daingean in the sixteenth century.

It's possible that someone might be under the impression that Ní Bheildiúin's imagination must surely be restrained by the centrality of the mountain in the poems, but that person would be mistaken. What the poet has achieved here is something quite special; not only has her mountainous muse not restrained her creativity, but the use of Cnoc Bhréanainn to root such a varied collection of voices, poems, and themes firmly in the landscape of the Kerry Gaeltacht has succeeded in proving, once again, that Irish poets can surely write of both the local and the universal, the near and the far, the modern and the historical, while dealing with the personal and political issues of life. One might be reminded of Cathal Ó Searcaigh's poetry, and of his beloved landscape of Mín a' Leá and Earagail in Donegal.

Ní Bheildiúin is clearly an accomplished poet, as was already evident from her previous collections: *An Teorainn Bheo* (2007), *Púca Gan Dealramh* (2010), and *Meirge an Laoich* (2013). It is certain that *Agallamh sa Cheo* is indeed a worthy addition to her own corpus, as it is to the Irish-language poetry corpus as a whole, and it is no surprise that Duais an Oireachtais 2018 was bestowed upon this wonderful collection.

If Ní Bheildiúin has employed the presence of Cnoc Bhréanainn in order to root her poetry in a certain place, it is within the minor events of everyday life that Doireann Ní Ghríofa weaves her own poems in her bilingual collection, *Lies*. This collection comprises a choice of poems from her previous Irish language collections, *Résheoid* (2011), *Dúlasair* (2012), and *Oighear* (2017), alongside translations of the chosen works. Since Ní Ghríofa is a poet who composes poetry in both English and Irish, it is no surprise that she herself has translated the poems, and that she has succeeded in creating distinctive translations that hark back to the original work, without being direct translations of same. It is also of note that the title of the collection, *Lies*, is in English alone, and that it is subtitled 'poems in Irish with English translations by the author', something that might well encourage the monolingual English reader to open the book.

These skilful translations should be applauded for their creativity and variety. An example of the poet's ability in this field can be found in the poem 'An Bróiste Rúiseach'/'The Russian Brooch', which is dedicated to Eavan Boland. The lines '… luíonn an bróiste Rúiseach a cheannaigh sí // ar chúig phunt i siopa seandachtaí' are translated to '… lies the Russian brooch she snagged years before, haggled // down to a fiver at an antiques stall'. No one could argue that the translation is a direct one, exactly, but the poet succeeds here in re-creating the sound techniques of the original in a new way. The rhyme of 'a cheannaigh sí/siopa seandachtaí' is reflected in the consonance of 'she snagged/haggled'. This kind of poetic transposition is seen throughout her translations in this collection.

Similarly to Ní Bheildiúin, Ní Ghríofa is not reluctant to play with style and form in her work. A good example of this is the poem 'Faoi Ghlas'/'Under Lock and Green', that breaks with the 'normal' layout of the poems in the book. The double meaning of 'glas' is also noted in the

English title, and is invoked very much in the themes of the poem itself; I was here reminded very much of the series of poems 'Na Murúcha a Thriomnaigh' by Nuala Ní Dhomhnaill, in the themes of water, memory, and submerged trauma. Ní Ghríofa uses, like Ní Dhomhnaill, the water as a way of discussing the trauma and memory of the woman in the poem: 'teach   tógtha ón uisce,   teach tógtha   as uisce'.

Like Boland herself, Ní Ghríofa constructs a mysterious world for her readers from the matter of ordinary life. The poems of this collection impress upon us that magic and depth can be found in the plainest minutiae of the everyday. This motif comes to us especially in the poems: 'Suburbia' / 'Suburbia', 'Brúitín' / 'Mash', 'Féin-phic le Línte' / 'Selfie with Lines', and 'Dialann na hOíche: Miasniteoir' / 'Noctuary: Dishwasher'. She often uses housework to discuss questions of history and ethics, and it is the poem 'Triptic: Obair Bhaile' / 'Homework: A Triptych' that best shows this tendency. Historical events such as the voyages of Vasco da Gama and Sir Ernest Shackleton are juxtaposed skilfully against the ordinary work of the poet around her home. Household items are also used to create a sense of wonder, such as in the poem 'Scragall Stáin' / 'Tinfoil', in which tinfoil is unrolled into a silver river in the home: 'Dhéanainn / abhainn as, lí mhín liath scaoilte timpeall an tí'. Imagination, history, and the self are all interwoven into the poet's daily work around the house, and the poems spring naturally from this source.

In *Agallamh sa Cheo*, Ní Bheildiúin gives us the opportunity to understand history, life events, and nature in the context of Cnoc Bhréanainn, the mountain that functions as a touchstone of time and place in the collection. In *Lies*, the poetry is rooted in the normal life of the poet and the person, as well as in the memories of Ní Ghríofa herself. The approaches of these poets are as different as could be, yet they both succeed in bringing the reader on a distinctive journey, through time, place, and memory.

Ann Quinn
Halloween Mansion (2017)
Oil on board, 30 x 25 cm

Ann Quinn
Impression of Isfahan (2014)
Oil on canvas, 100 x 122 cm

Ann Quinn
Summer on My Father's Farm (2018)
Oil on canvas, 100 x 80 cm

Ann Quinn
Don't Be Afraid (2018)
Oil on canvas, 97 x 122 cm

Ann Quinn
Derek and his Dog on Top of the Silage Pit (2017)
Oil on canvas, 70 x 100 cm

Ann Quinn
Joy (2019)
Oil on panel, 16.9 x 12 cm

This painting is currently in the summer exhibition at the Taylor Galleries,
16 Kildare St, Dublin 2, until 7 September.

www.annquinn.org

Chad Campbell

THE COLD

aches the window corner and sweeps the field.
Husks the milkweed, blues the corn, is after
the flint of your wrist with the same grey
tendril that slows sap in the quarter living
inch of wet laburnum. Call it fleet. Call it
the sense turning your head in a high wind
all this time someone has been singing from
the treeline. It winnows at the keyhole. Would
blow out the ember and sweep the dust of you,
who sits in the brittling heat of a cast iron stove
thinking the sky is so vast you had better
wrap your child in amber: brief in her bed
as the cold smell of rain on a stone.

Rachael Hegarty

ANNE BYRNE

There is a holy well near ours.
I will take our youngest there.
His eyes ain't the best and some say
there's a cure in Donagh's Well.

That's another job on me list.
The list of never-ending things
to do or get done. I want fun,
a different kind of list.

Not the one to fix broken bits
of second-hand furniture,
ditch chipped plates and cups,
or paint – a fresh lick for every room.

I want a day out, not shopping
in town for the needful –
the girl's Bay City Rollers knee socks,
or the little lad's Bionic Man jocks.

No, I want a day by the sea.
We'd take our kids to the secret beach
at the back of Howth Head.
The one with loads of steps down –

granite slabs edged with fern,
ivy, bramble or blackberry bush.
I'd teach them chiselers
how to mosey around nettle stings

or thorny scrawbs from dog roses.
How to catch a fresh breath
of sea air and mind tricky rocks,
wet shale or slippery wet moss.

I want us to take in the view
of the Baily Lighthouse.
I'd explain its beams of caution
needed on dirty, stormy nights.

I want me family to see the sea,
and the fact of a lighthouse
on a summer day, on a family.

*Anne Byrne (35): Housewife, married, Donaghmede, Dublin. Killed
in Talbot Street while on a shopping trip. Survived by her husband,
Michael, and two children: Michelle, aged 8 and Trevor, aged 4.*

Rachael Hegarty

MICHELLE O'BRIEN'S STATEMENT TO THE OIREACHTAS PUBLIC HEARINGS
ON THE BARRON REPORT, 20.01.2004

*I am the daughter of Anne Byrne who was killed on Talbot Street.
I speak on behalf of my father, Michael Byrne and my brother, Trevor.
On 17th of May 1974 our day started like any other. Little did we know
that by 5.30 p.m. that Friday evening our lives would change forever.
My dad came home at lunch that day to drop my mother into town.
My brother and I stayed at home. Our neighbour minded us. I
heard the three loud bangs as I stood in our house in Donaghmeade.
When Dad came in from work, we told him Mam hadn't returned.
Dad searched the hospitals. He found Mam's remains in the morgue.
He knew it was our mother because she had worn a green coat
and by her wedding ring, which I am very proud to wear today.
Mam was buried that following Tuesday, on my brother's birthday,
and to this day, my brother has not celebrated his own birthday.
You know, it took our father 15 years to walk up Talbot Street again.*

A.M. Cousins

DRESS

1979

The blue summer dress,
purchased in haste –
nine ninety-nine in A-Wear –
was woven entirely from viscose
with an elasticated waist
that facilitated the swelling belly;
gentle gathers at shoulder level
drew the eye from the ripening breasts
and the skirt skimmed the hips.
A pattern of scattered red pencils
made the priest smile when I walked to the altar.

Morning sickness struck directly after the vows
and the floor came towards me.

I remember some embarrassed laughter
when my new mother-in-law fetched water
from the sacristy and held it to my lips,
her steadying arm around my waist.
I didn't care much then.
I care now.

I care that I broke their hearts,
that, all those years ago, I made my mother cry
and my father may have cried too
as he shook his head because, even with a degree
under my belt, I was as foolish as the ones
who gave it all away for nothing and tried
to cover their tracks with corsets
that pinched and squeezed under wedding dresses.

The dress hangs in my wardrobe –
I check it every now and then –
the waist sags slightly,
the hem has been adjusted
to accommodate changing fashions
but the blue holds fast to its man-made fibres
and the interfacing still supports the collar.

Anthony Walton

PENNYWHISTLE

– Seamus Heaney (1939–2013)

Let the low notes
drone

like experience, steady

as they weather rock
and human faces, bring
the waves, shape
the sands, bend
and ripple the grass

up strands and estuaries –

the midrange stands
for the imagination

a steady melody and dance

of comfort
and the gentling
tasks of the everyday
the moments when
a maker might glance
at loved ones
and catch a breath –

that leaves the keening

register of cries
that cannot be controlled
or hidden, the sail

that becomes
the sky, the wind
and too high
for even the keener

to hear

Colin Dardis

PLAYING, CLOBBERING, GROWING

Matt Kirkham, *The Dumbo Octopus* (Templar Poetry, 2016), £10.
Karl Parkinson, *Butterflies of a Bad Summer* (Salmon Poetry, 2016), €10.
Maurice Devitt, *Growing Up in Colour* (Doire Press, 2018), €12.

Matt Kirkham enjoys playing about with form, as his previous sonnet sequence with Templar, *Aged Fourteen My Grandfather Runs Away to Sea*, testifies. The keystone of *The Dumbo Octopus* is 'Russian Dolls', a five-part sequence containing a sestina, villanelle, sonnet, quatrain, and haiku. Exploring a mother-daughter relationship, each element in turn cannibalises, using only the words of its predecessor to create an impressive exercise in reductivism. One can imagine it must have been hell to write, but the reader will appreciate the reward.

Alongside games of form, Kirkham favours the long sentence, layering and solidifying the subject, reminiscent of Bohumil Hrabal's *Dancing Lessons for the Advanced in Age* or Mike McCormack's *Solar Bones*. 'Yggdrasil' is one long delicious sentence over sixteen lines that never threatens to digress or shrink back. 'Poppies', another one-sentence poem, echoes the long calculations of Beckett's *Watt,* while 'Smoke' lets loose on the need for us to communicate, smoothly transitioning from Skype to smoke signals. 'Poem To Be Read In A Submarine' repeatedly pushes one thing inside another, building ideas of suffocation, claustrophobia, and being overpowered:

> The way a voice is wrapped
> inside a phone this begins
> as charged air wrapped in the sacks
> of your lungs wrapped in flesh
> wrapped in charged air wrapped in steel
> and its buoyancy wrapped
> in water-wrapped salt.

There is a faint suggestion of security within all these layers: 'in his belly a dunlin' matches a line from 'Topography', 'she gauges the drumlin of her belly', the image of a womb or cocoon counteracting any sense of threat. However, the idea that solace is to be found within familial settings flip-flops throughout the book. The poet clearly delights in his own family and parenthood, his children making many cameos throughout; but there is unease with a deeper, more ingrained generational positioning. 'The Rat' bemoans 'the dumb spawn of tinkers' and 'all my great-inbredto-the-power- / of-what-grandparents'. The Sick Sow 'pucks up the history', thinking of 'her mother's milk', its pastoral inheritance seemingly rejected. Both share Larkin's revolt of family values, with the awareness that the child, in Larkin's words, 'contains both of them'.

We see a literal representation of this in 'Reds', where Kirkham marvels over his daughter's hair colour, a combination from mother and father 'that almost demands / your out-loud cheer?' 'Green Plastic Dinosaur', the toy itself a symbol of the pratfalls of parenthood, is also a meditation on the ageing process. Its effective refrain varies on the idea of 'hopping, wavering, toppling, tumbling down', perhaps a commentary on how overwhelming parenthood can be.

The poems also use repeated symbols of water to create total immersion within a subject: 'dog heavy mist', 'polyphonic ocean', 'my voice is lost in the sea's rush', a sea that 'gulps down the night' – all of these help form a work that is overawed by nature and by life, equally aware of the beauty and the dangers contained within. This collection is the voice of someone who has found their bedrock, having reached maturity, but still containing a playful admiration with the world.

Butterflies of a Bad Summer is Karl Parkinson's second collection, weighing in at a slim forty-two pages of poetry. The offering is a mixed bag, catching the energy of his spoken word performances, but also littered with weak similes: 'beautiful as a slug', 'words still fire like a bullet in the brain', tears that 'run like the water of a dark river'. However, Parkinson can strike home with a cutting comparison or metaphor, such as in 'They Say "Kit" Marlowe Was A Spy':

> They hung a chain of names
> around his neck like a set of
> > bones:

> Brawler
> Heretic
> Homo
> Counterfeiter
> Magician

> I hope that he wore them like golden
> > amulets.

Parkinson seems attracted to celebrated misfits and mavericks, such as Marlowe. A large part of the collection is given over to exploring the lives of such historical figures and artists. 'A Love Letter To Reinaldo Arenas' is perhaps the most successful, closest to the essence of the character, rather than merely a recitation of life events. The poem celebrates Arenas's outspokenness – instilled 'with a panther's grace' – and sexuality, set in opposition to the Cuban Communist government who 'jailed you with murderers / because you were queer'.

Elsewhere, the character studies more often fail to capture the reverence and sublimity of the people they deal with. 'Superstar Simeon Stylites' focuses heavily on the image of the figure perched on his infamous pillar, without touching upon his motivations. Likewise, 'I Am Bodhidharma' captures some of the mystery and legend of the Buddhist monk, but falls flat when it becomes mere proclamation rather than illustration: 'I am raw, / I am throbbing, / I am a crazed teacher'.

The Beats also get a strong look in: Gregory Corso, Hubert Selby Jr, William Burroughs, Jack Kerouac and friends all appear, to wrestle with 'the funny striving we call our lives'. 'Killing Charles Bukowski' is full of blind praise, without any awareness of self-destruction, as if 'roaming the bars / of L.A. looking for a lay' was something grandiose to strive for. Elsewhere, Parkinson asks 'Blaise Cendrars / was a writer. // Are you?', as if you can only be a writer if you suffer horribly, like Blaise Cendrars getting his arm blasted off and gritting his teeth through the pain like a real whiskey-drinking man.

Such crude machismo culminates in 'Poem For My Body' – the poet proclaiming to be 'a pneumatic fuck machine' – and also perhaps influences 'Making Love To Frida Kahlo', where Kahlo is celebrated more as an imagined sexual conquest than for her artistic accomplishments. However, the poem given over to her is not without tenderness: 'You be the ground, / I'll be the rain'.

The writing is far stronger when Parkinson deals with his own experience, and the centrepiece of the collection is 'No More The Clopping Hooves Of Death's Horses In Your Legs', an elegy for a deceased friend. It is a contemporary counterpart to Auden's 'Funeral Blues', dialled up to eleven. The sequence superbly captures one's helplessness in the face of death – 'Shall I slice off both ears, so as not to hear the death / rattle's melody?' It is full of rage and disbelief, clobbering the reader with all five stages of grief at once. Yet there is remarkable tenderness too: 'lay his head on the pillow of gold … lay him down on bier of lilies / and pink lotuses'.

Pick up almost any collection by a male poet over fifty, and you'll find that ageing and the steady approach of death are favoured subjects. *Growing Up in Colour*, the debut from Maurice Devitt, is no different, except Devitt has managed to find a way in delighting in old age and the wisdom it allows, the poems containing the right mixture of childhood innocence and adult retrospection. 'Sinister' is a prime example, a reflection on a curious desire to be left-handed when a schoolchild. An attempt to trick a teacher with a makeshift sling and cries of a broken arm are met with a scolding from mother. Devitt balances invention – a rope ladder is pulled from a pocket in order to climb down the hole of a chalk-lined 'O' – with repercussion, what is described as the 'uniform chaos / of your teenage years' in the titular poem. Another marvellous invention imagines a swan mating with its napkin-counterpart.

Unlike Parkinson, who appears to suggest that poetry can only be found in greatness or in suffering, Devitt revels in the small things. A caravan in a field is a 'metal cow'; a person pushing a lawnmower looks like they're 'walking a really obedient dog'. You'll stop to ponder the clinical efficacy of phrases such as 'the bullying of the storm', 'the primacy / of colour', 'half-eaten silence', or 'shaky stillness'. Such language elevates these poems above where they are set, in the everyday and commonplace, and very much in the land of retirement:

> I sleep better since I curtained
> the louvre door, and wake
> to the joy of a blank diary,
> [...]
> and looking to cheat at Solitaire,
> while, every day,
> the postman cycles by.

The strong implication is that there is comfort to be found in this 'choreography of routine', even if sometimes it is a quiet comfort, or affected by limitations and issues of health. For example, a relative's golf and driving improve, oddly, after losing an eye ('A Speckled Life'). Such reflections on mortality inevitably lead the poet to consider his own father. 'A Story My Father Told Me' recalls the seven year old seeing Devitt Sr. scoring a goal, 'the first witnessed by me for posterity'. 'A Football Dynasty' traces another familial moment through the sport, with a 'well-rehearsed / monologue, delivered breathlessly / from the rocking-chair'. Both poems are subtle and tender, as indeed are the memories and sentiments throughout the collection, without ever becoming twee,

Amidst these fond memories, there are also darker notes: 'The New Neighbours' taps into the paranoiac sense of the unknown that feeds suspicion and xenophobia. 'Incident at Fallow Water' appears to lay the blame for a traumatic incident on a stranger 'who worked the farm, gentle hands, cap pulled down to hide his eyes'. 'Before the Storm' longs for seclusion and safety, but fears the 'eye / at the window'. Scattered amongst other softer pieces, these poems are better for their scarcity, a counter melody to the proffered caricature of a comfortable life.

Similarly, we also see signs of illness and frailty creep into the edges of this life. 'The Possibilities of Darkness' addresses dementia, with a Mrs Feinstein out looking for her husband who has passed, 'lost in the war, but which husband, / which war?' Devitt muses on what will happen to a favourite jumper after he is gone, mild anthropomorphism elevating the clothing to the status of a loved one who must face bereavement ('The Consolations of Wool'). The roles are reversed in 'Cornflower Blue', where a cardigan brings back memories 'like the reassurance / of a friend lost somewhere / in a crowded room'. The item is left 'casually / on a chair', as if its wearer might return to put it on again sometime.

The advantage of having a debut collection in your later years is that you have a lot to say, and *Growing Up in Colour* offers a lot for any reader to savour and enjoy. Out of these three collections, it is perhaps the most well-rounded, with Kirkham close on its heels, and Parkinson away from the pack, which is where perhaps, one suspects, he prefers to be.

David Murphy

BOLIVIA

The rim of the valley that shelters La Paz
hides hovels of El Alto where displaced hunters
sharpen arrowheads and roam high streets
seeking long dead empires.

Fathers sit on rows of empty gas cylinders
outside mud-wattle cantinas supping *cerveza*,
talking and muttering of Evo Morales
and tin mines of Huanuni.

In the city down below, Inca teardrops gather
in gutters and refuse to evaporate.
Young women behind lace curtains file their nails;
mothers in *pollera* skirts wrinkle up

their noses at illusory oil-and-gas money of
light-skinned suitors from eastern lowlands.
In downtown stalls old Indians sell axe-heads
as trinkets to *American Express* tourists

returning from 4x4 tours of the salt flats
and wondering where to next
– Machu Picchu, perhaps?
Is that in Brazil?

Simón Bolívar has a lot to answer for,
cobbling together a country diverse as a continent,
precious as pendant ice on the Altiplano,
fragile as coca leaves in the side of the mouth.

Hope clings like a swirl of *paja brava*
bending on howling plateaux, warm and soft
as the wool of a bounding vicuña hunted almost
to extinction, making a comeback now.

Dairena Ní Chinnéide

AN AIMSIR LÁITHREACH

– i gcuimhne mo mháthar

Tamall i ndiaidh
do bháis
braithim tú
san aimsir chaite
den gcéad uair
as láthair
i nduibheagán na marbh

níl agam ach taifead ded' ghuth
an ceol cruinn
a shil le meadaracht
thomhaiste do chuid cainte
ní raibh aon fharasbarr
ach cumarsáid bhinn

chuala tú ar R na G
d'ardaigh mo chroí
bhís san aimsir láithreach
ar feadh scaithimh
chríochnaigh an clár
d'fhéachas amach an fhuinneog

ag lorg rian díot
macalla do ghlóir
mar a bheadh leigheas
ón saol eile.

Dairena Ní Chinnéide

SOS MÍOSTRAITHE

Mo mheon
ina striapach
réamh-mhíostraithe

crochann cantal faobhrach
tharam ar nós galar tógálach
tinneas im' chíocha
rud éigin amh im' bholg

tá mo mheon crosta
ar tinneall chun catha
seachnaítear mé
ar nós sceach gheal

sula gcím braon fola
in aon chor
teannas marfach san aer
scian im' bhroinn

de gheit tagann sos
mo chorp saor ó dhaoirse
mo bhroinn folamh
an glas casta.

James Ragan

THE WEIGHT OF AN UMBRELLA

Before its slick vinyl could wing its carapace
out above the body's width of shoulders,

before the tin ribs could arch to challenge the air
it had displaced in the sudden lift of sky,

before the knobbed handle could power-up
the palm's easy grip of manipulation

to deflect the assault of an Arctic wind
or the full force of a child's fisted sword,

it had been a thing of furniture, hanging
as adornment off the carved oak stair

or the hook of a hat tree-rack.
Before I could legislate the crowning of a cap

on the hard breathing of my balding scalp,
it had grown to be a thing of need

like a walking cane or a tent restraining
the elements of a cloud's quick temper.

It had never denied its role in knowing
what history of wind or sun it had rejected,

what weight in swallowed drops it had to pay
to save the ground from the deep soak of grime.

You would think it might find a greater need
than saving such a brainless head as mine.

Kevin O'Farrell

THE HOUSE HUSBAND

I am hanging out alongside
pale ghosts of her work-week:

whenever they've finally dried,
I will gather them up gently,

then place them out of sight,
so her absence is less near to me.

Refusing to be obtuse
or still, as objects usually are;

they dangle slack-armed, loose,
these faceless avatars –

each collar now become a noose;
each cuff another ligature.

Philip Gross

A MODEST PROPOSAL

... and we'll build a house on the wind
whose almost weightless membranes flex
and ripple round us, like the flux
of light on water – a house of the mind

shared, minds together. So we'll rise
on our own thermal, fanned by sun-vanes
hushed as moth wings, as the trailing vines
of airstream dangle us, ripe fruit, and the rose

of the compass unpicking its petals – love
me, loves me not – at our feet, the known
world simmering with detail, vast and clear

without borders or ground-rent. We'll live
on the wind, in a sentence without nouns,
all verb: we'll be nowhere, everywhere and here.

Richie McCaffery

FALLING

He came from Felling and spent his life falling,
my Great Grandfather, Alfred Holden.

A reluctant corporal in the Border Regiment,
put on sniper-duty, he climbed a tree at Ypres.

Shot in the shoulder before he could take aim,
the fall saved his life, sent him home.

Later in a riveter's brace on the Tyne, he replied
to the Lorelei's call and plummeted from a liner.

He worked hard to bring his family up a peg,
but this made his drunken dive more spectacular.

They then put him somewhere where he could
fall no more but he'd already laced his gene pool

with a desire for descent. Sometimes I'm jerked
awake in the pitch middle of the night

by the feeling of free-fall. It used to scare me
but now I like the sense of weightlessness,

of being unburdened. Even the studio photo
of him taken on leave during the Great War

has a misty border to it, as if somewhere
he's plunging always through the clouds.

Grace Wilentz

STRUCTURE AND ENCOUNTER

Anne Tannam, *Tides Shifting Across My Sitting Room Floor* (Salmon Poetry, 2017), €12.
Luke Morgan, *Honest Walls* (Arlen House, 2016), €13.
Niall Bourke, *Did You Put The Weasels Out?* (Eyewear Publishing, 2018), €12.49.

Often developed over a longer span, first or early collections are rarely unified by a dominant structure or unified concept. These three new titles break with that convention. Displaying a strong awareness of the desired trajectory and impact of the collection overall, these poets appear to work backwards from that vision, carefully developing and selecting poems that serve an over-arching purpose: to generate momentum, drive a narrative forward, or simply open up a reflective space.

Six years after publication of her first book, *Take This Life*, Anne Tannam's *Tides Shifting Across My Sitting Room Floor* maps loss and grieving, navigating their disorienting effects. Though she chooses not to divide up the book, the reader has a clear impression of the poems splitting into two asymmetrical sections: those written before her mother's diagnosis and short battle with leukaemia, and those that come after.

Tannam's style has a strong forward momentum. Her lines are self-assured, even when she is struggling with the unreliability of perception. In the collection's earlier poems, such as 'Parallel Universe', there is the premonition of moving towards some unpredictable, transformative change:

> It happens unexpectedly.
> I might be walking into town,
> each house I pass in its rightful place,
> neat rows of apartments all standing in line.
> Then a gap appears, revealing space I'd missed before.
> Another dimension opens wide ...

The poet has described her process for developing this collection as recording a journey. And the sense of immediacy she creates is effective – we take the turns with her. Narrative and chronology are important in this collection. Tannam wants to tell her story, but she also revels in upending time and interrupting the unfolding narrative to delve back into memory, or to take us somewhere else.

Often in these poems, the boundary between past and present, interior and exterior, blurs and the reader is suddenly transported. In 'Land's

End', after the speaker resigns herself to weekly blood transfusions, the poem dissolves what separates the solemn scene from the sea beyond the window pane:

> Her words, the curl of the shore,
> the weight of the land, receding;
> a siren call—low, hypnotic—
> thrumming through your veins.

Tides Shifting Across My Sitting Room Floor meditates on loss and charts it with the eye of a careful documentarian. 'Undressing' traces her father's bedtime ritual, and the daily dissolution of his memories to dementia, using a clear, short line:

> Slowly he unbuttons
> brother, husband, father, son,
>
> slips them under the pillow
> for safekeeping,
>
> pulls back the covers,
> turns out the light.

The overall effect of *Tides Shifting Across My Sitting Room Floor* is that of a family photo album, its pages flipped forward, and back and forward again. There is something universal captured in the specific and the deeply personal. The reader comes away feeling that Tannam is working hard to sift lessons from all this loss so that she can share them with us, a worthwhile and generous project.

Luke Morgan's *Honest Walls* is a debut collection with a high degree of poise. It is well-paced and creates a distinct feeling of space. While there is a clear sense of voice and of a unified experience, the poet resists allowing a dominant narrative arc to emerge. His careful ordering of the collection instead allows individual poems and moments to shine through.

Morgan's strength lies in his delivery of a strong image, often captured in a closely observed gesture. When he succeeds, he reveals a new way of seeing, as in 'Conducting':

> When you heard
> for the first time
> on that trip to Mornington
> one of Beethoven's symphonies
> you moved your hands

out the window
and became its conductor.
You pulled the landscape
together and apart …

In 'Anniversary', the poem feels almost like a frame for the startling final image. The poem opens flatly, 'Today is no different. / Minutes are exchanged / like a currency', before becoming haiku-like in its unfolding into a striking visual moment:

In the sharp breeze
outside their window
the cherry tree crumbles
like confetti.

There is a careful economy of language in the most effective poems, where Morgan is both thoughtful and restrained. At times, his filmmaker's eye also reveals itself, as in 'Directions' where, at the side of the road, maps are drawn with hand gestures and lines in the dirt, before the perspective pans up to a bird's eye view just after all parties have departed:

Shukran, offered flatly
before you resume your journey,
the road tracks left behind
like two great arms outstretched.

Morgan was first published by *Poetry Ireland Review* at sixteen, and he dedicates his debut collection to the teacher who encouraged and supported his creative development. As a collection, *Honest Walls* is at its strongest when the voice is detached and observant, pursuing new and sophisticated ways of showing us what we have already seen; it is a debut that reveals no shortage of skill and potential.

Niall Bourke's *Did You Put The Weasels Out? – A Perverse Novel in Verse* is ostentatious about its form and structure, and also more densely packed. The poems are divided into 'The Arias' and 'The Remscéala'. Sonnets interplay with footnotes in verse, creating two distinct universes on the page.

Bourke stitches together a mock epic from these constituent parts. Its protagonist, Mark Setanta, manoeuvres his way through work and the city, back to his 'de-facto' wife with whom he thinks he has fallen out:

There are a few swells to climb
Yet. 1. Boozing since dinner time.
2. He may not have a job tomorrow

3. He cannot, just now, locate
His wallet (he is already on probate
For losing keys he'd borrowed).
4. It is quite late into the night
And no text sent since their fight.

As you might have noticed, the collection is stacked with allusions to the *Táin*, seeking to honour the balance the Táin strikes between the poetic and sheer bawdiness. A series of sonnets progress the narrative, occasionally punctuated by comedic performance pieces. One of these is 'Some Denizens', which takes inventory of the cast of local characters who remind Mark of 'why he left home':

> … your wan who lived only on cider and porridge for a whole year and contracted the first case of scurvy since 1837, that chap with the wife who looks a bit like a curtain, the poor auld Sniper's Nightmare who got polio when he was little and now zig-zags up the street, that quarehawk who sits on the wicker chair in the sweet shop muttering did you put the weasels out?

There are beautiful digressions, too, like the reflections of the Thames in 'River Retirement Blues':

> I was a working river.
> Liquescent envy of the world.
> But, weakly now,
> My weary smiles
> Meanders meek
> The many miles
> And I,
> A neutered tomcat, lie
> Sleeping round
> The city curled.

Did You Put The Weasels Out? is ambitious and imaginative, if demented in its obsession with form and structure. Though it seems primarily preoccupied with achieving a humorous effect, when not aiming for a laugh the collection can land real sentiment, sincere and clearly articulated.

Steve Denehan

DIVING

I borrow a breath and dive
off a rock, old as time
into lives I might have led

I taste the salt of goodbyes
of faded postmarks
of the fact that you don't care to notice now
the specks of dirt on your crockery

I close my eyes
feel the brush of carnival streamers
against my upturned face
muffled drums beat through me

the screech of tyres
the sudden stop
I am airborne, forever
then
I feel the grit, clawing, frenzied
into my chest

I am a ghost, resting on the ceiling
I watch myself below
withered and wheezing
sagging under a thin white blanket

I am burning from the inside out
and return, gasping
like I always do

Christopher Cusack

A PENNY FOR TWO THOUGHTS

I. IF NOTHING ELSE –

And then there was that Remembrance Day
when you mistook some uniformed bemedalled
chap for King George – and he long across the
river of woe. You, on the contrary, were still just
taking Lethe's water homeopathically: two drops
daily under the tongue, until your mind dissipated
and you followed. Your residual Mayo lilt, phonetically
heedless of current conditions, made your praise of this
English monarch stranger still, and altogether I could
hardly understand you, as if you were signalling from
a far-away Western hilltop, as if you had meandered
(as it were) to the other side of your valleys of youth ...
You were labouring hard to have me comprehend you
from across the chasm of this memory. It could hardly
have been a better joke if Elizabeth (First or Second –
either would have done fine) had turned her face towards
the camera, away from the Cenotaph, and from under her
hat-brim had responded to your generational faux pas in
kind, had addressed you by your grandson's name (mine)
or by some epithet for a Greek hero such as Odysseus
or Achilles, who like you both entered Hades but *did* live
to tell the tale ... Yet though formidable, she is not known
for her sense of humour. Was it a tribute to yourself, then,
shortly before you followed this dead ringer for George,
Rex Imperator, across the Styx? (Shrouded by mythical
personae, I tried to reveal some truer emotion.)
Had it been so, I would have cried, perhaps,
but it was too soon, and my eyes bled instead.

II. AND THUS IT CAME TO PASS

(British Library to British Museum, 0.8 statute miles)

"People seem to be very disciplined in this
room," or words to that effect, the speaker
some guardian of death, preventing books
that belong to later generations from being
removed from this Luxor, city of hereafters.
Strolling a little later past museum exhibits
tracing similar lines, I rehashed my thoughts
and reinscribed them upon the bandages of
Rameses-like gurners, gargoyles of desiccated
flesh, and some fey lad (Roman period) *aetat*.
XXI or so lying in state a few paces down. Here
were deeper meanings; here I must reflect on
the desire to detect truth in vestigial realities,
to divine immortal words from quotidian
figures, a truth of books & mummies: the
dusty loves of some poet, some lesser oracle
grasping for Rosetta words behind crowds,
in granodiorite, impeded by figures of speech.

Berni Dwan

I TAKE YOUR VIOLIN TO FREIBURG

You go a few days early, burdened
with the wardrobe of a twenty-year-old. I
follow later, weighed down with the particulars
of travelling with your violin; holding, carrying, resting
position; not dissimilar to taking your new-born-self home
from the hospital. I

hold it by the handle like I held you by the hand, taking you
to your first violin lesson; your four-year-old fingers eager to
become acquainted with GDAE – the notes that will provide
the back music to your growing years. Four years, four strings, endless
possibilities; the bow, your Harry Potter wand wielded with increasing
confidence. You bite your lip as you magically make music with horsehair
   on steel. I

clutch the case tightly as I walk through crowded train stations; convinced,
occasionally, that I am clutching your toddler hand, telling you to hold on
   tight. We
change at Stuttgart and Karlsruhe, arrive in Freiburg to be greeted by a smiling
   you.
We made it! We band of three, we happy crew, carry the precious cargo to
   your student flat.
Now, you will make music in Germany, from notation I cannot read, joking
   with fellow
players in a language I do not understand. With just four strings, you navigate
   a wider
realm, your calloused fingertips a testament to your determination. Tuned

anew in Freiburg, the resonance of GDAE lingers in our Dublin home. I
am a proud and willing messenger.

Erin Wilson

TRACKS DISAPPEARING OVER A FIELD

Late day bruise of clouds –
      does the sun love the world and show it most in its leaving?

Stippled fringe of conifer and a crosshatch of white birch,
      breath freezing around the collar into a stiffened mast.

It is a painted glass plate you walk toward that holds the ache like art,
      cows sheltering from cold in a copse of divested trees.

Queen Anne's lace, its lesser known sister-self
      (who warms to its skeletal presence?) – empty palm thrust upright.

A bus delivers a child home, late, maybe the last run of the day,
      to a dog's bark dying down in the distance.

A crow passes overhead and caws three times,
      a signatory to existence, removed, inviolable.

You carry inside of you an opening of possible hunger that sharpens
      as you move, a hot dinner heating the edge of this cold landscape.

Fox tracks leave the road, enter the field, then disappear.
      What does this warm red drum amble after? What could there possibly be?

Ann Leahy

A BLACKTHORN WINTER

The funeral done, we walked in bright, expectant April
on lanes that wound to the crumbling burial ground.
Ash trees, hung with last year's wretched seeds in tatters,
waved like beggars eager to converse. All we heard
was a rattle as the wind exhaled through each.

Too weak to stand, she'd seemed not desolate but amazed:
"imagine me, *me* who could fork reeks of hay drawn in
by men, *me* who could do the work of any of them?"
As if this day – her last – was the first on which she'd noticed
any change: decades had shrunk to a season.

Spring was stark. Blackthorn in arthritic tangles
occupied a nether region, leafless, yet pricked
with hard-nosed buds in pink, caught between
death and regeneration, as if the year
was loath to burgeon again within the bark.

By Month's Mind, roads were fringed with Queen Anne's lace
in frothy umbels thrust on thin, frail arms
to buffet every car that passed in futile gestures
of embrace. Petals clung for weeks like wings
ripped from death's spectral insects. Who could forget?

We'd stood then, sure of death, not sure when, while buds
on midnight's trees were seared with frost. And mutterings of love
perished, half-formed, as we composed ourselves by the bed.
At last, a gasp, then a pause. But who knows what shrill,
silent screech? What soft, billowing updraft? In the end, no words.

The graveyard's unkempt edge was faintly sibilant
by summer's close with blades of Yorkshire fog
that bowed before the wind's blunt scythe.
Then that dissolute breeze withdrew to leave
them leaning, not quite touching, hushed and askew.

Catriona Clutterbuck

HOLY

Holy is the bed they rolled your body on
from the Emergency Room to the one they set aside
for our last night together as one family
of father, mother and (just-deceased) child.

Holy the nurse who, when she banged your bed
against the door-jamb leading us in,
in deep reflex instinct for your sacred life
said immediately, "I'm sorry, Emily."

Holy the steps I took from my bed to yours
in the small hours to cradle your strange weight
and holy those that followed to your father's side
who warmed me through while I held your shoulder blade.

Holy the arrival of my sister and my brother
early next day to help us to the city mortuary;
holy the mysteries of the nurses' skill
who made you flexible again for that last journey.

Holy your uncle's upper body strength
who carried you tenderly to the hired car
and placed you in our arms across the back seat,
face to my chest and your hips to your father's.

Holy the sunshine on that early Sunday morning
on the old man sitting outside his front door,
and every quiet word exchanged between us two
as the driver sped along those empty roads.

Holy then, the texture of each of your bare feet
in our last moments with you after arriving,
as one by one, I slipped from them the white socks you'd put on
and covered you with the blanket they'd provided.

Holy at the last the arms that held me up
outside the door I had to leave you behind,
as holy, holy, holy now and always are you –
our beloved, our darling only child.

Kate Miller

DAY OF RECKONING

My neighbour Chantal used to lead the choir.
We sang the *Dies Irae* with her only months ago.

The funeral, this woeful day, *dies illa* – part in anger,
part in disbelief we thunder through the requiem

for the departed. Let everlasting light shine, *lux perpetua
luceat*, on those who've gone before.

Mors stupebit et natura. I was thinking of my daughter.
Death will marvel as will Nature

when they clap eyes upon my daughter.
I still see her in the garden, thirty-eight forever.

Death cannot age her. She never wears the wig we bought,
her breasts look perfect.

As she will be, *dies illa cum resurget
creatura*, on the day that all creation

rises up to meet its maker, *rex tremendae
maiestatis*, for whom my own dead

Mother's voice descants – a high sweet voice
before the doctors burned her vocal chords –

she was not much more than a girl herself
and she could really sing.

Caoimhín Mac Giolla Léith

FRÍD DHORAS NA BHFOCAL

Cathal Ó Searcaigh, *Crann na Teanga / The Language Tree* (The Irish Pages
Press, 2018), €30 hb.

Is beag file Gaeilge de chuid ár linne a bhfuil stair níos casta ag roinnt lena
'iarchatalóg' ná Cathal Ó Searcaigh. Ní hé an leabhar seo an chéad
iarracht – ná baol air – ar rogha shuntasach dá dhánta a sholáthar do
phobal na Gaeilge, ná go deimhin do léitheoirí an Bhéarla ach oiread, ó
d'imigh 'Gúrú na gCnoc' i mbun pinn nach mór leathchéad bliain ó shin.
Is cinnté, áfach, gurb é is tathagaí. Breis agus ceithre chéad leathanach atá
anseo againn, iad roinnte ina rannóga faoi rúibric na gcnuasach aonair de
réir mar a foilsíodh iad, ó *Miontraigéide Cathrach* i 1975, nuair a bhí an file
fós sna déaga, go dtí *Teanga na gCorr*, a foilsíodh anuraidh. Tá dornán de
'dhánta na hóige' (1970-1980) anseo freisin nár foilsíodh go dtí 2005.

Más file é an Searcach nach leasc leis filleadh ar dhánta a chum sé i
bhfad ó shin le coigeartú beag a dhéanamh anseo is ansiúd, is file é freisin
atá sásta an deis a thapú i gcnuasach den sórt seo athmhúnlú áirithe a
dhéanamh ar éabhlóid a shaothair thar na blianta. Mar shampla, tugann
an rogha anseo, ó na cnuasaigh luatha go háirithe, le fios go raibh an toise
hómaéarótach atá i réim le fada anois ina chuid filíochta lárnach ón tús –
luaitear 'an grá crosta' agus 'an grá séanta' láithreach sa chéad dán anseo
istigh – gné nach mbeadh chomh follasach céanna dá mbeadh a mhalairt
de rogha i gceist (mar a bhí i bhfoilseacháin inchomparáide dá chuid
roimhe seo). Ar ndóigh, tá scríbhneoir ar bith i dteidil pé leagan de féin
is mian leis a chur faoinár mbráid de réir mar is toil leis.

Níos minicí ná a mhalairt nasctar ceiliúradh na collaíochta le ceiliúradh
ar áilleacht aiceanta a cheantair dhúchais in iarthuaisceart Thír Chonaill.
Baintear leas coitianta as an tróp seanbhunaithe i gcultúr na Gaeilge trína
samhlaítear gnéithe den tírdhreach mar chorp daonna – corp leannáin go
hiondúil – agus a mhalairt. Níl file comhaimseartha Éireannach is mó a
thugann ómós seasta dá dhúthaigh dhúchais agus bíonn feidhm nach mór
sacraimintiúil ag Sliabh na hEaragaile ina shaothar a chuirfeadh Mont
Sainte-Victoire Cézanne i gcuimhne, nó Sliabh Fuji i bhfilíocht agus in
ealaín na Seapáine. I dtús a laethe mar fhile chaith an Searcach tamall ina
chónaí i gcathair Átha Cliath agus i Londain, tréimhse a spreag glac dánta
frithchathrach atá inchurtha le dánta den dul céanna le Máirtín Ó Direáin
tríocha bliain roimhe. Tagaimid anseo ar 'glas-stócach an tsléibhe / ar strae
i dtoitcheo na cathrach ... agus ansiúd / san áit is uaigní ina chroí / ag cur
snas ar a sheanchuimhní; / ag déanamh dánta as a dheora deoraíochta'
('Deoraíocht'). Murab ionann is an Direánach, áfach, is fada anois ó d'fhill

Ó Searcaigh ar a bhaile sa Ghaeltacht, fág sealanna i Neipeal agus in áiteanna eile i gcéin, faoi mar is dual d'fhilí a ghlúine.

Dála aos dána a ghlúine freisin bhain an Searcach brabach ón tús as an soláthar scóipiúil a rinne foilsitheoirí an Bhéarla, Penguin go háirithe, sna seascaidí agus sna seachtóidí i dtaca le saothar nuafhilí an domhain mhóir. Ait go leor, níl trácht ar bith anseo ar aingeal coimhdeachta Uí Shearcaigh i measc filí na haoise seo caite, Constantin Cavafy, bíodh go bhfuil dánta tiomnaithe do scríbhneoirí éagsúla mar Osip Mandelstam, Isaac Rosenberg, James Wright, Jack Kerouac, Máirtín Ó Direáin, Máire Mhac an tSaoi, Michael Davitt, agus Gréagóir Ó Dúill, ní áirím cairde iomadúla eile nach iad. Téama sonraitheach is ea feidhm na filíochta agus cúram na teanga, iad araon lonnaithe go daingean i ndúchas an bhaile: 'I Mín a' Leá / fríd dhoras na bhfocal, siúlaim / amach asam féin' ('Altú na Maidine'). Más inbhéartú é seo ar línte deiridh 'Fill Arís' le Seán Ó Ríordáin – 'Sin é do dhoras / Dún Chaoin faoi sholas an tráthnóna / Buail is osclófar / D'intinn féin is do chló ceart' – is idirghabháil choinníollach idir Auden agus Yeats atá sa líne '*Anseo* braithim go bhfuil éifeacht i bhfilíocht' (liomsa an bhéim) ón dán aithnidiúil 'Anseo ag Stáisiún Chaiseal na gCorr'.

Tá éagsúlacht na filíochta anseo, ó thaobh foirme de, le moladh go mór. Mar sin féin, is fearr ar deireadh an Searcach, dar liom, nuair is fuinte, mar atá sa liric ghleoite seo a leanas:

TAOBH THIAR

Ní ardaíonn tú i do shuan
Aon tearmann ná daingean

Le linn na hoíche bím ag siúl
I do shaol laistiar de mheall na súl

Atá níos dúchasaí ina ghoirme
Ná sais na Maighdine Muire.

Ar an taobh cúil d'fhocail
Tá a mhacasamhail de shaol.

Nó a leithéid seo:

CUIBHRINN

Tchím os cionn bhinn
na mara cuibhrinn
ag sleamhnú le fánaidh.

Ach ab é na caoirigh
atá ina suí orthu, á dtromú,
mar mheáchain ar pháipéir,

d'imeodh siad le fán
ina nduilleoga glasa
síos isteach sa duibheagán.

'It's the rare poet who can imagine sheep as paperweights who keep the fields from blowing away', arsa an file Meiriceánach Billy Collins i mblurba ar chlúdach an leabhair agus ní díol iontais lé leis an dán áirithe seo a bheith ag file mar é a chleacht ariamh stíl ghlic chumarsáideach neamhchas.

Dá mbeadh corr-locht nó laige le lua roghnóinn féin iomarcacht na huaime anseo is ansiúd agus tútáil an mheafair róshaothraithe thall is ab-hus. Tuigim, mar shampla, gur d'aon ghnó an dul thar fóir sa dán 'An Lilí Bhándearg' agus an file ag tóraíocht 'Focla a bheadh beacht, braiteach, beannaithe, briathra bithbheo / a bhéarfadh brí agus beatha / do mo dhán', ach ní hionann tuiscint agus maithiúnas. Agus ní mé a bhfuil aon slánú i ndán dá leithéid seo de bhladhmann ón dán próis 'Lá de na laethanta': 'I bhfíordhuibheagán na bhflaitheas thum mé *sponge* mo shamhlaíochta is nuair a d'fháisc mé é ina dhiaidh sin filíocht a tháinig ag sileadh as.'

Paddy Bushe a sholáthraigh formhór mór na leaganacha Béarla, atá ar an ardchaighdeán is dual dó, agus an file féin an chuid eile. Spéisiúil go leor, bíodh go mba nós ariamh d'fhilí na Gaeilge (in Éirinn agus in Albain) claonadh i dtreo na litriúlachta nuair a bhíonn Béarlá á chur acu ar a saothar féin, i gcodarsnacht le cuid dá n-aistritheoirí eile, a mhalairt d'fhonn a bhíonn ar an Searcach scaití, ar chúiseanna éagsúla. Cion ar im-eartas focal, is dócha, a bhronnann 'Let's Hit the Road, Jack' mar theideal Béarla ar 'Do Jack Kerouac'; agus tóir ar leathrím, b'fhéidir, a dhéanann 'Hitching between Glenties and Doochary / on a raw winter's morning in the 1970s' as 'Ar an ordóg idir na Gleanntaí agus an Dúchoraidh / maidin ghlasliath gheimhridh i seasca a naoi' sa dán 'Bealach an tSléibhe'.

Tá leagan amach neamhchoitianta ar an leabhar sa mhéid is nach gcloítear leis na ngnáthnós i gcnuasaigh dhátheangacha an bunleagan agus an t-aistriúchán a bheith os a gcomhair amach tríd síos, sa gcaoi is gur féidir leis an léitheoir dátheangach an dá leagan a chur i gcomparáid gan stró. Ina ionad seo tugtar an bundán Gaeilge ina iomláine, fiú i gcás dánta fada, agus ansin an leagan Béarla ar na leathanaigh a leanann, rud a dhéanann cúram na comparáide eatarthu pas beag níos útamálaí. Miong-hearán faoi mhórdhíolaim é seo, áfach, ar deireadh. Agus an uile ní ráite, is fiú a lua gur údar dóchais agus comhghairdis araon go bhfuil dánta áirithe ó na cnuasaigh aonair a d'fhoilsigh Cathal Ó Searcaigh le blianta beaga anuas atá inchurtha le seoda luatha a bhain áit amach dóibh i bhfad ó shin féin i gcanóin na nuafhilíochta.

Pippa Little

A FATHER IS

A father is a curiosity of birds' eggs
unstable in light

to be touched only with exhausted bristle
never exposed to water

a father is an antlered head
from the Tableau Hall

nostrils swabbed, eyes dusted
teeth burnished softly

a father is an old bird's nest
swelling inside the chimney

where moths will graze
and be smoked out by funnel

also a liver-pink coral
growing a starry mould under glass

a father is a death watch
that grinds through words

leaves what's left
in grey ash circles.

With thanks to *The National Trust Housekeeping Manual*

Marcus Mac Conghail

ATHFHOGHLAIM AMHRÁIN

Is gairbhe mo mhéireanta anocht, is righne;
Is gairbhe, is doimhne mo ghuth;
Is leisciúla mo theanga
ná oíche a chéad chumtha

Mo bheola ag baint blas na húire
de na focail
Ag foghlaim séis an amhráin aríst
– cúinní ceoil a dhorchaigh

Scafall an mhéadranóim ag rá
Moilligh Séimhigh Rithimigh
Brúigh ag an stiallóg go cruinn
Pioc gach sreang go beacht
os cionn an fhuaimphoill
Muirnigh an muineál
—coimeád an chabhail teann le do chorp féin.

Ó C go G go mion A,
is an corda is deacra dom—an F damanta sin
Ordóg do na dordbhuillí,
—tribil ón lúidín, ón sisile

Guth agus seinnt ag imeacht le sruth
Focail sa bhfraoch, nótaí caoch orm—Foc!

—tosnód aríst

Beidh sé agam an uair seo, a Ghrá.

Marcus Mac Conghail

GAN FOCAL

Gan focal gan friotal
gan idirghabháil idir dhá theanga
gan cuimhneamh ar cé leo a bhfuilim ag caint
gan timpeallú gan mhaolú ná canúnú ná faic
ach ag dúnadh mo shúile is ag análú isteach
—ag folmhú m'aigne de dhaingneáin fheistithe
Gan gá le gearradh trí stiallacha tiubha fada plaisteacha
a dheineann ionad dorais a dheineann réscaipeadh ar sholas
idir fuarsheomra stórais an bhúistéara
agus seomra tosaigh an chustaiméara
Gan gá le tuin chainte a thomhas
—titim na bhfocal san ord is cóir
—rithim an fhriotail de réir mar is ceart
de réir pé rúibricí atá ceapaithe ceadaithe faomhaithe réamhshocraithe
Ach corcra—braithim corcra
—daba míchothrom éagruthach sa chúinne
braithim ladhracha fada buí ag síneadh go himeall uaidh
braithim cuar donn ag imeacht áit éigin
braithim stiallacha den pháipéar á stracadh ar chúis éigin
braithim saoirse braithim sruth
braithim glóthach braithim glae
braithim sileadh braithim úscadh is púscadh mótúil
braithim spúnóg adhmaid ag cuimilt is ag scríobadh
—ag fuineadh comhábhair i gcoinne shleasa an bhabhla
braithim dathanna is cruthanna gan bheola gan bhrí agus braithim
tuiscint ag teacht ón tost atá ag téachtadh
—foc focail anyway

Gary Egan

REASONS FOR REJECTION: ALTERNATIVE PREJUDICE CHECKLIST

Not because s/he is a traveller
but because the poems roam,
reluctant to settle on a tone or theme.

Not because s/he is a different nationality
but because I don't understand
the hell where this poet's coming from.

Not because of her/his religious beliefs
but because s/he refuses to worship
the same poetic deities that I do.

Not because the poet's a single parent
but because s/he isn't married
to the tradition I want to perpetuate.

Not because of her/his sexual orientation
but because of her/his sexual frankness
and slowness to condemn deviance.

Not because the poet is elderly
but because her/his verse forms are old-fashioned
and consecrate an antiquated philosophy.

Not because the poet is handicapped
but because s/he uses form as a crutch,
leaving content without a leg to stand on.

Not because s/he is neurologically atypical
and presents with profound learning difficulties,
but because the poems are intellectually challenging.

JS Watts

My first reaction is panic.
Damn! Where's my camera? The telephoto lens?
But despite my frantic flutterings
it isn't to hand.
No point cursing my lack of foresight,
the yellow gold of the autumn's afternoon
is barely waiting.
I give in to now, let the frenzy fly on,
leaving me and my luck at field's edge
with two tranquil buzzards paired in flight
mere feet above my eye's camera.
Close enough to view each crescent moon
spanning the closest wings,
haunting white against rich russet,
dark beauty barring each splayed tail,
to feel I might reach up to touch,
tip to tip, the splayed ends of those strong-fingered wings,
to see a keen black eye
peering down through mine,
fixing the image of the moment
against a sky-wide world
framed only by the field's loose embrace
and human limitations.

Grace O'Doherty

SIGHT / SEEING

I go back to that street and the sunshine.
Tourists alight from coaches
with cameras strapped around their necks,
children and dogs dance
in the fountain in the park
to fifties jukebox hits
from the funfair rides

and the yellow-haired lady is on my mind
who reads palms in her caravan
and walks with stiff hips to the shop
each morning for milk and bread and probably
tea leaves to read, her old trade,
dependent on people who need
a forecast for personal weather,
for a dark stranger to appear in their lives,

I walk again beside these pedestrians,
these seagulls
and the bleached dead crabs on their backs
the tide keeps leaving behind,
they are falling out of my hands
and I splay them on the table
in a half-circle,
I tell myself: now choose.

Katie Donovan

I'm sorry,
you can't be a poet any more –
you aren't young or sexy now;
or even a beautiful person
whom everyone online adores.
You haven't had a lover in years
and your children are teenagers.
You look alright – but not in photos –
and worst of all
you're so peggable as a mum.
That's you in the supermarket, right?
hovering over spinach
dreaming up a nice school lunch?
You should be slumped
over espresso in some NYC lookalike café,
or drinking wine as you pen
another lyric to heartache.
Stop thinking about feeding the birds
and paying the heating bill.
Don't eat any more chocolate,
and, as for cheering your son on
while he plays soccer –
have you totally lost it?
If you could have just frozen yourself
circa 1995, when you wrote that one poem –
you know, that ended up
by freakish chance in *the* anthology? –
you might have managed
to remain a viable presence
on the poetry scene. But now,
well, truth to say (unless you're prepared
to give a reading for a fund-raiser –
would you be? for free?)
you're just a has-been.

Martin Dyar

ANIMAL MAGIC

Gail McConnell, *Fourteen* (Green Bottle Press, 2018), £6.
Eoghan Walls, *Pigeon Songs* (Seren Press, 2019), £9.99.
Joe Dunthorne, *O Positive* (Faber and Faber, 2019), £10.99.

Gail McConnell's pamphlet of poems, gathered under the unfussy title
Fourteen, provides evidence of a special talent on the way to a first full-
length collection. 'Narwhal' and 'Worm' are poems that look at animals,
in special modes of curiosity and strangeness. The worm in 'Worm'
receives a kind of instruction on the subject of its oddness, its industri-
ousness and its ancientness. In effect, the creature is ventriloquised, and
the resulting image is at once an identifiable thing and a compelling index
of a broader biological world. Both the imaginative trick and the written
product appear very natural. Even as the poem applies frames of sensory
experience to the imagined centre of the worm's life, in lines such as,
'Eyeless, your appetite aerates', and the remarkably sympathetic 'You
ingest to differentiate', the tightness and lightness of the language, and
the thinking behind it, maintain the sense of a mind accessed through
poetic substance.

McConnell's worm displays consciousness without appearing as
something merely or solely humanised. And this might be characteristic.
In *Fourteen*, eco-centric insights work to undermine anthropocentric
foundations. There's a channelling perhaps of Ted Hughes, with parallels
to Hughes's hyper-terrestrial eye. But no mere discipleship or emulation,
or for that matter eco-poetic pride, holds McConnell's writing back.

The poem 'Narwhal' indicates more of the poet's range and commitment in her pursuit of a human-animal continuum. 'Narwhal' – there is
a slighter poem of the same name in the second half of the pamphlet,
which extends the subject playfully – presents again the living, breathing
animal in subtle and solid visuals. This individual whale is a being defined
by routines, abilities, and endeavours, which together provide the terms
of its own perfectly strange existence. There are touches of commentary
on scientific limitation, coupled with stabs at what human reason might
not entirely grasp in the whale's world. But when the last line turns back
to the human, there isn't a sense of anything calculated, and no limiting
of the poem's thrust to what a reader might more readily identify with.
Rather, there's a memorable and teasing sense that the truth of human
life is partly revealed in holistic approaches to the earthly existence of
unearthly creatures.

The poem 'Octopus' is an impressive development of the technical
dimensions of 'Worm' and 'Narwhal'. McConnell has found the key figure

of her tidy bestiary here: an endearingly weird creature, digging for a framework of language to account for the riddles of mind and neurology that are the octopus's calling card.

Like the worm, the octopus is addressed in human terms as a means of sketching out the wondrousness of its life. The re-use of this device, when reading these poems together, leads to a sense that the animals that are being spoken to are being ushered towards a fuller form. There's a delicate note of pity too which deepens the vision. The octopus is informed:

> All you know you know by touch; shape,
> texture and scale you draw into
> the mouth of every flowering cup.

These words suggest an elaborate effort by an elaborate body. And they are linked to further nuance and purpose when the poet suggests to the octopus that this way of being reflects a desire to have 'a chance to draw a body not / your own into your care'.

That word 'care' implies some of the power, poise, and special intent of *Fourteen*. In the last verse of 'Octopus' there's a deep question: 'Attachment: is it grace or grasp?' What follows is not so much an answer to that octopus's poser, but an acknowledgment that the truth must entail some species of wholeness. In, as it were, an animal's shoes, the reader can for a moment attempt to be at one with a submerged power: 'All things unknown familiar in / the peeling off & letting go.'

In the poem '*Urvertrauen*', in Eoghan Walls' excellent new collection *Pigeon Songs*, a daughter has had a frightening encounter with a dog. This intrepid girl is not unfamiliar to the reader. In 'The Tooth Burier' she has already played an allegorical role in a meditation on life and death. In 'Swimming Lessons' she has been a figure of unwitting grace, an elemental angel half-transformed into an animal. Later, in 'Nettles', her pain will offer a dilated view of life on earth. These effects relate to key tendencies in the writing. In *Pigeon Songs*, the light of parental love is rarely cast without a filter of mortality, just as the wonder of childhood is never viewed as being entirely distinct from the wonder of life itself.

These leanings animate a poem titled 'The Weight of Her', where the daughter sings out a series of innocent reflections on how death might be overcome. To get by in the underworld, she'll need to have, naturally, 'her own dead horse, a patchwork nag / of bones and worms to bear her past the zombie dogs, // or if her tights get caught, she'll only have to whistle, / and he'll whinny over to prise her from the brambles'. A father is listening to these beautiful plans while carrying their maker on his shoulders, the weight of her increased by the irony of his being, for now, her real and trusty steed. But Walls quickly locates the limit of the game.

The father struggles, recoiling from the memory of an acquaintance who lost his daughter. By being anonymous, that other man, 'Mr S', brings another infusion of feeling to this expertly shadowed poem.

Darkness evolves in '*Urvertrauen*', where the contrasted destinies of a human daughter and an orphaned hare are considered. Universality is worked into the litany of things that serve to distract the daughter from her distress: 'the fear of death-by-dog and her bloodied knee // fade to enlightenment in the glow of talking pigs, / Coco Pops, or gestation periods of dinosaur eggs'. While the familiarity and wryness are a treat, and a fine quotidian poetry, they are a ruse too, and the poem's second half advances unstoppably into the grimness of the leveret's fate. The hare daughter has evaded the dogs, but she watches 'as greyhounds rough up the carcass of her mother, // whose only shield is stillness'. There's another view of life here. The leveret is being initiated by nature, and it seems that the instinct of fear which preserves her might entail a means for her to carry on, however vulnerably:

> As her blood dries,
> she holds the branching horizons in her wide eyes,
>
> learning her atheism in the thorny greys of the sun,
> flat on the mud where she'll feed and fuck and run.

There's a more than acoustic emphasis on the *her* of 'her atheism'; we go back to the poem's opening again, and to the contrast in question, which now seems to be a matter of parallels. It's almost as if the human daughter, by being reassured, is at the same time being disconnected from reality, from the animal basis of her humanity. The words 'basic trust' are suggested in the German title, but the poem might have its doubts.

'Notes on Repin's *Easter*' is outstanding. We meet the hare again, an agent now in the recruitment of Jesus Christ for ecological purposes. The voice of the poem incorporates a subtle detachment, mimicking a gallery catalogue ('Note the hare's red jowls', and 'Repin notes …'), but the primary approach, beautifully contained, stems from a hearty iconoclasm. The final line presents a kind of triumph: 'The greys in Christ's beard are the hare's greys.' We have journeyed from religiosity down a chain of being, past human concerns, and into a place of alternative and seemingly truer divinity.

There's impressive range in *Pigeon Songs*. 'Kepler-22b' handles illness and medicine and astrophysics together, keeping lyrical and personal intentions in tune with a striding evocativeness of diction. 'The Pale Child' revises and enhances a theological stance with existentialist vigour, the verses clipped, and the lines clean and speech-like, with no loss of philosophic urgency. 'Sisyphus in Laytown' impresses for its vision of courage in isolation, its straddling of literature and happenstance. 'The Pigeon on the Rafters of the Station of the Metro', part of the great sequence of pigeon poems in the book (each of which sensationally pushes past the lowly status of the bird), documents yet another pursuit of that supreme environmental fiction: animal experience. Walls, it should not be doubted, has the ability to deeply conceive and map out such flights of imagination, and to offer them on the page with singular power.

Joe Dunthorne occasionally goes for representations of animal consciousness in his compelling first book of poems, *O Positive*, but, in keeping with an involved exploration of doubt, particularly doubt with respect to being a poet, his more serious lyrical moments are very often interrupted.

The opener, 'A Sighting', is a wryly framed, fantastical narrative about a bear appearing in a campsite. The first words, 'as we waited to be torn apart', in their excess, connect us to the last line, where a macabre note pushes the diction beyond true fear or violence, and the effect is deepened by the inclusion of a spiralling train of thought.

The speaker recalls not exactly what happened in the near miss, but rather what they, in their lucid panic, apparently thought might be going on in the bear's mind just before he pardoned them and left them alive: 'I remember thinking the bear / looked like an actor in a bear suit / who had quit his frontier theme park.' Importantly, such playfulness and the emotionally oblique approach it reflects are not the full substance of the poem. Within a demotic register, verbal extremes flash in and out, and chords of wonder are struck firmly and suddenly. The speaker imagines that the bear recognises, in the way the tent's groundsheet is being spread out, a form of 'absolute devotion'. There's further resonance in the impression that he is a creature dwelling among broken oaks, and that he believes the frightened human protagonists are 'playing at language and marriage'.

There's distinctive poignancy here, parcelled with poetic openness in miniature, but there is also a thematically relevant refusal of a full embrace, something which chimes with a closing line later in the collection: 'I gave each object its soul, a word I rejected, of course.'

Relatedly, the poem 'I wanted to see how unhappy I could get' pursues a persuasive alloy of fluency and impediment. A handful of expected words is cut from the narration, giving a sense that the descent into unhappiness has had certain neurological consequences: 'My life was hopeless when it was. I had the thinnest skin since sliced.' These bruised statements are treated with forms of vision; and it seems that the unhappiness is not to be given free rein. The following line, for example, reflects an entrance of beauty into the cool surface of the poem: 'Then God in the shape / of a young professional paused / her soft commute.'

At the end of 'I wanted to see how unhappy I could get' there's a sense of temporary breakthrough, an escape from the urban grind and some luck for the unhappy quester: a 'garden square that was open to non-residents just this one day of the year'. This image of minor freedom prompts a signal of cognitive renewal: 'And there / I thought of other words for the little bitty sticks / of grass that were not leaves or blades.' This representation of a poet's wrestling with the experience of poetry itself extends to forms of poetic identity in poems like 'After I have written my important poem' and 'In which I practice happiness'. In the latter, Dunthorne writes: 'I hate the bit of the poem where you're obliged to hate something.' Against this putative distaste, the poem's close tapers downwards in a beguiling rage for positivity:

> I love the piano.
> I love true crime.
> I love the sun
> when it arrives
> like a tray of
> drinks.

Infectious and ingenious shorter poems like 'House Guests', 'How are you co-worker?', and 'Worship', represent a finer, less literary palate, while the memorable 'Promenade', 'Sestina for My Friends', and 'Workshop Dream' suggest that the poet's interest in ambivalent versions of the poetry life might be connected to a single theme; namely, over-exposure in milieus that are packed with aspirants. And yet, again and again in O Positive, conviction and originality march over the traps of angst and second-guessing.

Ciaran Carson

WILLIAM NICHOLSON, BALLROOM IN AN AIR RAID, 1918

The weather has taken a turn. Thick cloud cover, impending rain.
        It makes you consider
What it must be like to be the occupant of the sub-cloud car —
        a small device
Shaped something like a bomb, with an open cockpit, stabilizing
        fins and a rudder
At the rear. Consider it being lowered from the bomb bay of a Zeppelin
        at the end of
A 3,000-foot cable attached to a winch — the airship cruising safely
        out of sight
Inside a cloud bank while the crewman aboard the sub-cloud car,
        dangling some
Hundreds of feet under the clouds, directs the bombing via
        a telephone.
Consider the look, the weight, the layered textures of his outfit:
        thick woollen
Long underwear; standard blue flight coveralls; leather overalls;
        felt overshoes over
A pair of standard boots; leather gloves lined with sheep's wool;
        a lined helmet
With goggles; and a scarf. Consider London with its domes, theatres,
        temples; consider its skies.

Now consider William Nicholson's *Ballroom in an Air Raid* —
        no ballroom
In actuality, but the two-storey Masonic Temple located in
        the sub-basement
Of the Piccadilly Hotel. Such a cavernous space, concourse
        or antechamber
To the Underworld. Consider the rolled-up red carpet snaking
        from one end
Of the floor to the other that is a dark portal. Figures emerging
        from or loitering
Before it, some of them more shadow than discernible. Others
        aimless. Two

Stand out as officers by the cut of their cloth and their stance
        but ill at ease.
A stray chair stands at an odd angle. A woman sits on the carpet
        with a small child

Face down in her lap. A baby lies on the carpet in front of you.
Two women sit
In the corner, each with a baby in her lap. One of them looks out
at you,
The viewer. Consider the dirigible indiscernible in the bank of cloud
above Piccadilly.

from *Still Life* (The Gallery Press, 16 October 2019)

Ciaran Carson

JEFFREY MORGAN, HARE BOWL, *2008*

His gift revealed itself — a little book-sized still life
        of a bowl on a shelf —
Spongeware, 1850s — biscuit fired, says Jeffrey — decorated
        with a cut sponge,
A daisy chain of little blue flowers along the rim, and
        under them two hares
At full stretch running off to the right on the curve
        of the bowl. There'd be
Two others on the other side you can't see. Like the flowers,
        they're a faded blue, as is
The grass at their feet. Or is it shadow ... When we think
        of the painted hares
we think of the hares that have entered our lives,
        however fleetingly.

The hare on the runway at Aldergrove airport, seen as you
        came into land.
The hare that crossed my path on the Milltown Road, hedgerow
        to hedgerow in
The blink of an eye. The hare that stood and looked at us
        on Rathlin for an age.
The hare that you saw in your garden in Antrim, as tall as
        the child that you were.
So we go back to when we never knew each other, never
        dreaming then that we
Would end up in this here and now. We look at the *Hare Bowl*,
        then look at
Each other and smile. All day it draws us back to look at it,
        and look at it again.

That was then. This morning you've taken the bus into town
        to buy Easter eggs
And chocolates, and I'm left to contemplate the *Hare Bowl*
        on my own. It looks
Good upon the mantelpiece, propped beside the vase of daffodils
        we bought as
Tight green buds two days before, and now have opened up
        a blaze of yellow.
But I want to see the picture in a better light than this;
        the living room

It's in is dark, and the electric's always on. So I bring it to
        the parlour — facing south,
It gets the sun from dawn to dusk. I rest it on the back of
        the old overstuffed sofa

In the bay window. The muted colours suit the faded peachy pink
        of the fabric.
It's a few minutes after noon, and the grey drizzle of earlier
        is lifting a little.
I raise the Venetian blind. A cool pearlescent light streams in.
        There are textures
In the painting that I hadn't seen before. The bowl itself is
        resting on
A terracotta-coloured shelf, little flecks of red in it, the left-hand
        corner of the edge
Signed 'J·M' in red. Discreet. You have to look for it. Then I want
        to talk about the bowl,
But I'm distracted trying to put words to the green of the wall
        it's placed against.

How many shades are mingled there from pear to sage
        to olive green? Now
That I look at it, is there a background hint of yellow? Then
        I notice the lemon
Of our experiment, that's been occupying all this time
        in the parlour on
Its Moroccan saucer. We binned the banana when it went black.
        As for the lemon,
It's ever so slightly beginning to shrink and wizen, but still
        holding firm after
Three weeks — firmer in fact than fresh. In any event
        it glows against the green
Of the wall, the earth of the shelf, and the blue and creamy white
        of the bowl.

I'm wondering how Jeffrey got that illusionistic craquelure effect.
        So I email him;
He emails back. 'With the surface all wet and with a small
        Winsor & Newton
No. 7 sable brush (these are still licked into shape by old women —
        what happens when
They die — that's it) I paint the craquelure directly into
        the wet paint, then

Go to eat and watch *Newsnight* — it takes a week to dry.'
        A car horn sounds.
I look out the window. It's the usual crowded parking,
        morning surgery hours —
The Antrim Road Medical Centre is only five doors up
        Glandore Avenue from us.

I'm often there. *Was* there earlier this morning,
        getting an advance blood
For tomorrow's treatment at the City. In fact we're waiting
        to be seen there now.
The neutrophils are up to par, so everything is good to go.
        Here comes the nurse
With the cannula trolley. She ties the ligature, palps my lower arm
        to find a vein,
Then, head down, that look of utter concentration —
        Vermeer's *Lacemaker* —
As delicately, slowly, she works the needle in. *Cannula* the Latin
        for a little reed,
Or maybe a pen — the needle a nib with chemo ink to overwrite
        the faulty DNA.

Ninety minutes later we're out of the hospital. You call Fonacab,
        90333333,
You remember when we called it the Five 3s? Forty years ago
        or more ...
The city centre's gridlocked, according to the cabbie — an ambulance
        wails by —
Says he'll try the Westlink — we pass the Royal, where
        four years ago
I had my cardiac procedure — triple bypass, mechanical aortic
        valve — at last we
Reach the Antrim Road: past the Waterworks, and all
        the cherries suddenly
In bloom! And we're both so looking forward to seeing
        Jeffrey Morgan's *Hare Bowl* again.

from *Still Life* (The Gallery Press, 16 October 2019)

FEATURED POET: CAITLIN NEWBY

Caitlin Newby was born in Los Angeles and received her BA from Vassar, where she won the Beatrice Daw Brown Prize. She was awarded a Ph.D. in Creative Writing at Queen's University, Belfast. In 2018 she was shortlisted for *The White Review* poetry prize, and in 2019 she was named the Inaugural Bookfinders Chair of Creative Writing at the Seamus Heaney Centre. Her debut pamphlet, *Ceremony*, was published by The Lifeboat Press in June 2019. She is currently Poetry Editor of *Tangerine*, a magazine of new writing based in Belfast.

In *Ceremony* – a striking, eloquent short collection – and in the two poems in this issue, Caitlin Newby's poetry clearly tracks the instability of the idea of home and the shifting markers of identity. But the lines achieve a real lyric edge and reach that keeps the tone away from conventional elegy.

'Eggplant', for instance, the first poem in *Ceremony*, is a forceful, off-kilter account of a homecoming. Nothing is right. Nothing adds up. The poem ends with the bleak, reductionist line: 'it must be home because she's longed for it'.

In the elegant, dark poem here, 'Water', the speaker is not ready to find any emotional model in water. None at all. To imitate water, the speaker says, would result in being less not more:

> would be to wear myself thin,
> to be nowhere and nothing
>
> to no one – to be, in a sense,
> so much fickle weather.

The poem 'This Place' also re-states the exile from location: 'The view is stunning, / yes, but the view / reminds me of another'.

Displacement is a strength of these poems. It leads in *Ceremony* towards interesting translations of the visual landscape of painters – Chagall, Modigliani – but the centre of the themes and tones is always an implied disjunction between self and the outside world (place, seasons, elements), – the latter never exactly offering security to the former. It all makes for a strong destabilizing lyric work that draws the reader in.

– **Eavan Boland**

Caitlin Newby

THIS PLACE

you say, is nothing
but the view –
an empty bay
in the evening,
small boats resting
on their keels,
wet sand rippling
with the orange-
pink-blue-grey
of a sun sinking
behind distant hills.
The view is stunning,
yes, but the view
reminds me of another –
of further hills,
of mountains, even,
always snow-capped,
always hemming in
the horizon,
and of another bay,
where the grey-
blue line of the tide
inches inland,
where driftwood
chokes the shoreline
and herons wade
in the ankle-
deep shallows.
If I stepped beyond
the breakwater
and looked down
I could see almost
the same mud,
small rocks
and empty shells,
almost the same
always-changing
passage to the sea.

Caitlin Newby

ON WATER

You tell me to be more alive,
as water is alive. A wellspring,

a fountain, a fluid thing. But to be
so expansive, so mutable,

would be to wear myself thin,
to be nowhere and nothing

to no one – to be, in a sense,
so much fickle weather.

I could not be ubiquitous
or always kind, could not lavish

you only with my one living self,
but must be sometimes scarce

and sometimes dangerous
like all aqueous things, like love.

Benjamin Keatinge

SOFT KNOCKS THAT SCHOOL A LIFETIME

Michael Hofmann, *One Lark, One Horse* (Faber and Faber, 2018), £14.99 hb.
Harry Clifton, *Herod's Dispensations* (Bloodaxe Books, 2019), £9.95.

The English game of cricket has often puzzled visitors to the UK,
especially if they are not versed in its intricacies. In Michael Hofmann's
new collection, the poem 'Cricket' describes a dispiriting visit to Lords
where both the poet himself and his German father, novelist Gert
Hofmann, were underwhelmed by both the English summer and English
sporting traditions. It is 'Another of those Pyrrhic experiences', he writes,
'an ex*pyrrh*ience' in which a 'long-drawn-out' draw is witnessed between
'two mid-table counties' who are 'going nowhere'. A sense of jaded
defeat pervades the poem, as the game grinds on, and the on-field action
consists mainly of the ground staff bringing on the covers to shield the
pitch from yet another rain shower:

> One groundsman – the picador – mounted on a tractor,
> others on foot, like an army of clowns, with buckets and besoms.

With self-deprecating humour, an English farce is played out on the field
that has none of the 'finesse, economy of movement, timing' of a high-
level cricket match, a one-day international or a Test match. This is a
Dad's Army of 'clowns' and incompetents whose 'failing styles of drying'
only arouses a 'hearty' but 'malicious' laugh on the part of the spectators.
Meanwhile, 'Papa had his beer' and 'wondered' about this spectacle.

One might be tempted to see here *in nuce* the bemusement of
continental Europe watching British parliamentarian-buffoons capsise
their own country out of misguided hostility to the EU: Brexit played out
at Lords. Indeed, this intuition is affirmed later in the collection by the
poem 'The Case for Brexit' in which Hofmann recalls his UK childhood
in the early 1960s, which consisted of standard British schoolboy fare:
'School uniforms, playground fights. Goalposts. Polar ghosts. British bull-
dogs.' 'I should have liked to be called Roger or Arthur' the poet confides,
but in the 'winter of '63, the Plath winter', Hofmann would only 'bat for
days without scoring a run', his German accent mistaken for 'a serendipi-
tous knowledge of Welsh'. In the poem, British identity seems to
resemble 'a suicide pact'.

Hofmann considers himself to be German although he writes in English.
His relationship with his father and, by extension, his German background, forms the substance of two major collections *Acrimony* (1986),
winner of the Geoffrey Faber Memorial Prize, and *Approximately Nowhere*

(1999). One learns in these earlier collections that a certain degree of 'Ostranenie', estrangement, even 'pandemonium' characterised their relationship ('Baselitz & his Generation'), and forms a 'long and hopelessly trammelled backstory' ('Fontane') to these new poems. In the younger Hofmann's case, the 'Soft knocks that school a lifetime' ('Cricket') included boarding school, a childhood and adolescence located 'approximately nowhere' ('Directions'), and a cultural and linguistic bifurcation in German and English at once enriching and disorientating.

Even if the gladiatorial aspects of the father-son face-off have receded in *One Lark, One Horse* (the 'picador' groundsman of 'Cricket' seems more Don Quixote than Oedipus), this latest collection has lost none of the 'glum power' that Helen Vendler attributed to the poems of *Acrimony* in the *New York Review of Books*. And there are plenty of barbed hooks here too. On the political front, Hofmann's 'Letter from Australia' draws on the twenty-four-hour global news cycle to take some well-aimed swings at:

> Cheney the sinisterly skewed orang-utan,
> the worn charmlessness of Bush,
> the clumping one-armed snowman McCain ...

'Sarah P., the driller killer', and Republican Vice-Presidential candidate in the 2008 US Presidential election, fares no better a few lines later. There's a certain raw, but rather blatant, not to say brash anger at play in such obvious political critiques, not unlike the demotic rancour of 'Masque' with the refrain 'The government is fucking a corpse', in *Approximately Nowhere*. Elsewhere, Hofmann's jaded sense of late capitalist drift is less rhetorical and more sociological, if no less trenchant. The 'Sankt Georg' district of Hamburg is described as 'questionable, doubtful, shady, twilit', beset with 'drugs' and 'transients', 'whores and winos' but nonetheless, subject to 'the advance guard of gentrification'. The seediness is all too evident, but one sometimes wonders if the layers of glum description are laid on a bit too thickly. Hofmann has said in an interview that he loves 'those poor despised things adjectives' arguing that, if well-chosen, the descriptive word can be 'galvanising'. At the same time, such pile-ups as 'interchangeably frippish hideousness' and 'immediate, somehow always slightly grubby or compromised view' in 'Sankt Georg' seem to err on the side of gratuitousness. And there is, to this reader, a masculine bravado in many of these 'Pyrrhic experiences', but sometimes the bravado is in danger of drowning out the more nuanced tones of political and social *tristesse* which cohabit the same verbal spaces. The 'male discriminations' in these poems seem still preoccupied by the father/son anxieties of the earlier volumes ('My Father at Fifty', in *Acrimony*).

The 'knocks' in *One Lark, One Horse* also include middle-age and the accumulating sense of a bruised and battered self. 'Broken Nights' echoes

Philip Larkin's 'Sad Steps' as Hofmann patronises his '#2 bathroom *en bas* ... / Groping for a piss / As the poet saith' ('Broken Nights'). This most literary of poems is full of both literary bric-à-brac (Larkin, Lowell, Tennyson, the medieval religious lyric) and domestic bric-à-brac ('digital microwave', 'wireless') which are jump-cut together in a dense, postmodern patchwork of allusion and disillusion. Here, however, one feels neither the full desolation of Larkin in 'Sad Steps' nor the implied transcendence 'for others' outside the poem in Larkin's concluding vision of:

> ... the strength and pain
> Of being young; that it can't come again,
> But is for others undiminished somewhere.

The Hofmann poem, on my reading, lacks Larkin's hard-won authenticity, but this may be Hofmann's own strategic intention since he has said that his poems tend to retain 'this shimmer of inauthenticity or anxiety' because of his German upbringing and his extensive and award-winning work as a translator from German. If so, there is a strange medley here, it seems, of confession and craft, an alignment which might earn this and certain other Hofmann poems the epithet of 'inauthentic candour' or 'candid inauthenticity', with 'candour' being the very un-English quality that Hofmann has also identified, in a different interview (with Paul Bailey), as being part of his German heritage.

Hofmann's glum candour is further in evidence in 'LV', marking a mid-fifties birthday and signifying for the poet 'The luncheon voucher years', with the prospect of 'stiff joints' and 'small pains' and increasing 'listlessness' and 'irascibility'. However, Hofmann's litany of decay includes items that the hermit of Hull would definitely not have put on his list: 'Dino Buzatti's *Tartar Steppe*', or 'a nod to Franz Josef'. If Larkin seems to express partly a Yeatsian rage against physical decay and death, Hofmann's sentiments seem closer to lugubrious and unsentimental indifference. And perhaps there is a tonal continuity here that draws on his gift for reportage in both the political and personal realms. 'LV' might almost be paired with 'Silly Season, 2015', which itemises the political woes of that summer, most of which are still afflicting us:

> Countries not busily pursuing their dissolution (UK, Belgium) harden themselves.
> Walls go up against Serbia, Mexico, Palestine.
> [...]
> The weather breaks records every which way
> [...]
> The Chinese stock exchange gets all kittenish at a cost of trillions.
> America is good for an atrocity a week ('gun violence'), and doesn't get it.
> Brazenness or apology: a style choice. Putin is a figure from Artaud or Genet.

If there is an emotional force-field to these poems, it sometimes seems to be delimited – deflected, even – by their documentary methods. By prizing 'description' and by 'registering how the external world and its denizens sounded and felt', as Stephen L Burt puts it in the *TLS*, the poems reach towards an irreality in the real, a found surrealism. The chilling image that concludes Hofmann's early poem 'Nights in the Iron Hotel' where 'A gymnast' on an hotel TV screen 'swings like a hooked fish', is a prime example. Hofmann's latest poems continue to mine this rich seam of 'socialist realism for drunks' ('Nights in the Iron Hotel') in engaging, if sometimes circumscribed ways.

If Hofmann and Harry Clifton might appear, at first glance, to be poets cut from different cloths, there are nevertheless some useful points of comparison in their respective careers and outlooks. In his Ireland Chair of Poetry lecture on 'Writing the Rustbelt in Britain and Ireland', Harry Clifton helpfully surveys an array of British poets (Don Paterson, Ian Duhig, Sean O'Brien, but not Michael Hofmann), publishing in the 1980s, whose poetics bore witness to Thatcher's Britain – the 'cultural clutter of brand names and icons' of London, its materialism, the privatisation of intellectual life and of the universities (a theme highlighted by Hofmann in 'Higher Learning') – and whose 'social criticism' resounds in more archly political ways than perhaps the glum power of Hofmann's early poetry does. Clifton, as ever, writes as an astute observer of the scene, a participant who prefers to maintain his distance from the fray. Indeed, Clifton's new collection, a typically wide-ranging one in thematic and geographical terms, contains a humourous sketch on a reading 'At the White Night Café', in Chengdu, China alongside the 'legendary Ms Zhai', the 'doyenne' Clifton tells us in an *Irish Times* piece on his adventures in China 'of what was known as the "Misty" school of poets':

> A poet of the Meo tribe, smoking weed,
> Ignores me, ostentatiously [...]
>
> Professor Chan sits down. I see John Wong
> Stealing, surreptitiously, anything he is able,
> From the uncleared plates [...]
> Xu translates. A travesty, all wrong –
>
> But who will care?

One might imagine a not dissimilar scene in many a poetry café where egos are large and audiences often small. Indeed, Eleanor Goodman notes in a 2016 article on 'Women in the Contemporary Chinese Poetry Scene' in *Poetry Review* that China has more than its fair share of 'notoriously self-promoting, grandstanding characters' and mostly male poets who constitute, in Goodman's view, a distortive 'old boys' network'. Ms Zhai, we presume, is the exception, but the poet and translator Huiyi Bao is also an important presence in Clifton's new book, a cultural mediator who helps Clifton navigate 'the disparity between a Western mindset and a Chinese mindset' (Eleanor Goodman, 'I Let My Significance Happen Only at Home: Women in the Chinese Poetry Scene'). Clifton seems out of his depth in the White Night café, lost in the spotlight, where the 'Inspired misunderstandings' of the occasion 'Are crowding in' on him. Somehow, it all ends well, in an anxious comedy of errors.

The comedic mode, however, is atypical. These new poems from Harry Clifton are bestowed with characteristic philosophical gravity. But their weightiness participates in largely telepathic modes of communication which humanises them and often charges them with an emotionally direct pathos. The poem 'Daytime Sleeper' is a 'Gnostic' message sent across time zones, 'Ballinafall, 3 July 2014' elegises poet Dermot Healy (1947-2014) looking for an 'eye opening' in the mortal predicament, 'The Pit' is a not-so-innocent poem which evokes Herod's depredations more than his 'dispensations'. The poems communicate with their dedicatees and their subjects. But they do so, as it were, across the ether, across time and space. Indeed, Clifton seems to have hit upon the same conception as Hofmann in his adoption 'of Chinese feeling. Man in space. A bundle of memories and feelings and senses in a vast void' (Michael Hofmann, in Talking with Poets, 2002). These poems engage with hard rather than 'soft' knocks: death and art, suicide, history, loss of friends, ageing. But they cut through the mist, like a fog lamp, with their own sharp-edged clarities.

For Clifton, China provides not just an unfathomable cultural and linguistic complexity on which to brood; but in a more radical sense, it is a land of contradictions, an *entrée* to an ancient culture that has embraced hyper-modernity, 'an urban, rationalistic and political east and [a] mountainy spiritual west' as Clifton wrote in the Irish Times. This diversity finds expression in some remarkable poems that explore European encounters with China: 'Auden in Shanghai', 'Anabasis' (with Saint-John Perse as distinguished poetic precursor), 'Zhoukoudian' (with Jesuit philosopher Pierre Teilhard de Chardin witnessing 'the rise of Man, / The death of God', in the 1929 discovery of 'Peking Man'). There is an ambition here, an intellectual range and dexterity which, in Clifton's hands, becomes a renewed poetic spate that returns us to the muddy waters of world history that preoccupied him in his award-winning collection Secular Eden (2007). As Teilhard de Chardin perceived while 'digging deep in time' at the archaeological site at Zhoukoudian, these are realms that take us 'into the heart of Reality', poems that are the 'one in a billion chance' which must elude nearly all of us.

Glen Wilson

THE SEED FIDDLER'S BROADCAST

I calibrate the lever to tune it up,
setting number two sows six pints
of Clover Seed per statute acre.

These rills of Tyrone's heaped earth,
these depressions to be filled,
loosen in anticipation of seed-song.

Oil the journals and grease the stick well.
There is much to put in before life yields,
this is the rendition of many seasons.

Set the machine to your walk,
these fields are the audience,
every inch waits to hears me play.

My steps disturb the surface,
just enough for the future to reverberate
in the clearance of the past.

I scatter the seed like notes of a scale
until all the soil sings with this music
the harvest will be all beautiful refrain –

Keep your seed clean, keep the belt tight.

Note: lines in italics are taken from the instructions for an
'aero broadcaster and seed sower'

Sophie Klahr

SONNET AT A MCDONALD'S DRIVE-THRU ON A 14 HOUR DRIVE

I cannot write about America
without writing about race. Every glass
of water I drink is political.
What happened in geologic time once
now happens in lifespans. The president
misspells a word. _____ # of children
die in a school – the gunman is always
a man. I can't draw an accurate map
of any country. My grandpa's country
has now been erased by borders. I thought
of him for years only as *my mother's
father*. Unrelated to me. Sometimes,
a glimpse spilled from her: as a child, he played
in dusty streets with a ball made of rags.

Bernie Crawford

MISSING

I miss my cupboards, miss my shelves,
my dresser drawers, even the doors,

miss the roof, the windows, the walls of home,
the pictures on the walls,

miss family meals when the taken-for-granted sat as lightly
as reflected light from the small water glasses on the table,

when my child could leave a bruised peach on her plate
and reach for a sweeter one from the yellow bowl.

I miss singing familiar rhymes with my children at bedtime,
drawing curtains tight to keep the darkness out.

I miss my children. I keep a picture of the three of them
in my mind.

I miss my violin, miss the cat. She fled that first night
the bombing started.

I miss my books, scanning the book shelves
to find a companion for the fading evening into night.

Miss the gold cushions on the sofa. I worried their tassels
undone as they bombarded my city, again and again.

I miss the silvery green of the olive tree by the back door,
miss the smell of rain on parched ground, the smell of rain

on jasmine, the smell of sunshine on jasmine, miss
the taste of plump olives plucked fresh.

I miss stepping into the garden early in the morning,
stepping into the garden late in the evening

while the rest of the house sleeps, safe in their beds.
I miss being safe in bed, being safe.

Iulia David

SAINTS

Love is late Sunday at lunch,
all the family around the table, saints
at the top of the teaspoon handles
coming to life with warm pie –
the table's old pine,
the chairs are smoked oak,
they don't talk to each other,
four brothers bowing their heads
before their father, a necklace of gods
come to earth as themselves –
they're passing the tray around,
thick fingers, palms, coarse
as the crust on the pie,
where's the wine to wash away
the aftertaste of childhood –
the wine is over and the cold blood
orange juice rests in stains –
no wonder the dog shares
the melancholy of the leftovers,
unrestrained as they are,
with bare bones and pickles
and heart-shaped plums –
there's a vestige of busyness
between the blinks of the candles
one of them asks, another replies,
yes, it's already half past four,
then silence again. Another one turns
the radio on and a sad song dunks
the afternoon light in the sugar kitchen,
blue lino meets blue tiles,
a baby snake about to be born
in the corners of their eyes –
it's only a matter of time till one
will fight the other, these kind people,
who put the suckling pig on its bed of apples
with their hands and peeled the potatoes
with their hands, always on the lookout
to slake the ravenous thirst handed down
from the first to bear their name –

when there's no more wine,
they go for more pie, always,
always keep their mouths busy,
not to drop from between their teeth
the name of the one who died –

Paula Meehan

THE POET AS WRITING FELLOW IN RESIDENCE, TRINITY COLLEGE DUBLIN, 1992

This is the first in an occasional series of retrievals from the archives of
Poetry Ireland Review. *Paula Meehan's essay first appeared in* PIR
36 (Autumn 1992), edited by Peter Denman.

My first night on the job in the small bedroom with the narrow lumpy
mattress, I dream a dream that with minor variations usually accompanies
any new phase of work in the world: a towering institutional building,
very like the Reichstag, tiered seating filled with uniformed guests, mostly
men, all watching a lit podium, expectant. I'm outside putting my blue
pages in order. *Outside* is a twisty country road, potholed, rainswept. A
huge wind then and the pages are ripped from my fingers. A panicked
scramble in the rain, in the wind, to retrieve the speech or the poems or
whatever the pages hold from the ditches, the thorn bushes, the puddles.
I end up with torn and sopping shreds of blue, the print all run. Back at
the Reichstag, which I can still see into, the serried ranks are growing
impatient, muttering, shuffling. I walk towards the door, the lit podium.
As usual the dream dissolves there. I wake and it's dawn and utterly quiet
in Front Square; a clear mild January morning and I eat my first breakfast
on the window seat as the College comes to life.

The Fellowship is jointly funded by Trinity College and the Arts
Council, and lasts for six months, January to June, the growing span of
the year. I am given very fine accommodation (a huge living/work room,
tiny bedroom and kitchen), £5,325 as a stipend payable in six monthly
instalments, taxed to the hilt unfortunately, and the run of the College.
I can eat free at Commons and hear the grace-before-meals still offered
in Latin to Elizabeth and James, become a member of the Common
Room Club and avail of their wine cellars and gigantic armchairs, use
the library and its facilities (which include satellite link-ups to the other
great libraries on the planet), have my washing done by a lovely Dublin
woman in the best launderette in the world, and, perk of perks, I acquire
a Postern Gate Key. This latter means I can nip in and out of the mysterious doors that dot the surrounding walls of Trinity. When I was a small
child I got them confused with the open sesame doors of fairytale, and
something of that potency of magic threshold clings to them still.

In return for these creature comforts I'm linked into the School of
English under the kindly guidance of Terence Brown. The stipulated
duties are not backbreaking – I've to conduct a creative writing workshop
with candidates for the M. Phil. in Anglo-Irish Literature, another with

participants drawn from outside the walls, give a public reading of my work, and be available for consultation to students with an interest in creative writing.

I'm just not prepared for the level of that interest. Before long I'm struggling against an avalanche of manuscripts. For perverse reasons I expected the university to be exempt from the island-wide phenomenon of unprecedented literary activity. Pure prejudice on my part, but I thought there'd be the odd student dabbling in verse, and myself on the pig's back with long vistas of uninterrupted concentration on my own navel. Not a bit of it. Stories, poems, filmscripts, plays, novels in progress, journals, essays, and cross-genre mutations I've yet to find names for, come flooding in, mainly from undergraduates, and not all of them students of literature, or the humanities. In short, the vitality and enthusiasm and sheer productivity is akin to what you find now all over the country.

In my first term I end up conducting three workshops – one for the M. Phil. students and two for undergraduates. The M. Phil. students take the work very seriously; they will be assessed and graded on the basis of their finished portfolios. The undergraduate workshops are more laid back; they're there by choice, uninhibited by any notion of me as a judge. We meet in my rooms on Front Square, there are plenty of remedial pots of tea, it always seems to be wet and the light failing outside, and the gas fire sputters in the silence when a poem has been spoken or a story finished. If I had a charm for them all it would be a charm of arrogance – the world has enough devices to grind them down and the work itself will teach them humility if they keep on writing. But the getting-through skills for these times of isolation, of doubt, of the confusion of the maya, of the politics of this terrible century with its betrayal and corruption – what charm against the daily? A charm of arrogance and a hard neck. We are all searching for critical distance, to see the poem or story or whatever as *other*, to cut the umbilical and see if it has sustainable life of its own, if it can survive its maker, live in the indifferent universe.

That first term I got into Mountjoy once a week to work with women prisoners, mostly women who for one reason or another are victims of the great smack epidemic that has gripped certain communities since the eighties. I'd have once said working-class communities but the notion of a working class is long gone. Most of the women are from the same area I grew up in, the north inner city; a couple of them are from the same street. It is not hard to conclude that if you have a certain address you are most likely to end up, if you're going to end up in *any* institution, in Mountjoy rather than Trinity. I could be conducting workshops with students for many a long year before I'd meet someone from my own background.

Each time I go back to the students and look into their young and beautiful faces, I think how in a few years those who do not emigrate will occupy positions where they have power over the lives of children of the prisoners – as teachers, social workers, legislators, businessfolk. Another charm I'd wish for them: compassion, a social conscience.

It's Trinity's 400th birthday and it's one long party. Event after event to celebrate. A kind of party fatigue sets in after a while. The speechifying, the robéd processions, the fireworks, the theatrics, more speechifying. In the middle of all this the Miss X abortion controversy hits the national psyche a wallop. Everything changes. Forever. Another kind of procession hits the streets. Banners, chants (*Keep your rosaries off our ovaries! Not the Church, not the State; Women will decide their fate!*), a floodtide of anger. I meet some of my students on the marches. In the workshops there is much discussion of the misuse of language. One young man (who was a nipper when the Constitution was amended) proudly proclaims he's *Pro-Life* and brings me very flash full-colour brochures from some deep south US fundamentalist outfit. Bloody, frightening stuff. *Life Incorporated*, they're called. He tells me Father Marx visited his secondary school and showed him a video of screaming fetuses ripped from their mother's wombs. It's left a huge psychic wound. I lend him my copy of Brendan Kennelly's *The Book of Judas*. Maybe that'll help him heal before he's ever placed in a position of power over women.

The term ends. Peace and quiet and lengthening spring days. I can lose all sense of time, of myself, in my own work. I see few people: Kay who comes in once a week to hoover the rooms, Geraldine Mangan in the School of English office who is the kindest, most helpful and gentle spirit within the walls, the odd visitor. I begin to dream again, or at least to remember what I dream. One soothing dream I love: I'm writing with an ash twig in the sand by an ocean and I'm happy to have the waves wash the marks away: there is plenty more sand, the sun is warm on my face, not a sinner for miles, maybe not a sinner anywhere. Myself and the sea and the beach wiped clean again and again and again.

The new term brings with it another flood of manuscripts, this time for the workshop-in-the-community which is held in the cool blue rooms of the Writers' Centre on Parnell Square. Anyone in the city can apply. There's a postal strike, so I've to ring up all the people who've submitted work, twelve of them with good news, the rest with rejection. There's no getting away from it; they feel rejected – for all my explanations that my decisions are not a reflection of the quality of their work. Normally it'd be a cold white formal letter but now I'm at the end of the line and the vulnerability of writers is breaking my heart. I wish there was another way that didn't involve an implied value judgement. I wish I could take everyone, or pull twelve names out of a hat. All I can do is trust my instinct that a workshop would be useful to certain writers and that they can offer each other a pooling of skills and vision. We meet over the course of six weekends, the finest weekends of the year; though we don't know it at the time – there'll be no weather to match it for the rest of the summer. It's a real pleasure for me; my work is made easy by their commitment and enthusiasm and the absolute concentration they bring to the sessions. Most of the participants are women, a reflection of the submissions received, which were mostly from women. The *Field Day Anthology* storm has broken by this time. (*Not the Church, not the State* ... the spring chants come back to me – another side of the same coin). At my most despondent I'm grateful that so many women are writing; maybe one or two will worm their way into the canon so our daughters will have maps to guide them through their lives. At my most optimistic I think who the fuck pays any attention to these guys with their red biros and mealy-mouthed pontifications on culture – the tide has turned and they'll be left stranded on islands of their own misogyny where they'll dolorously bellow into their dotage, and by the time our warrior daughters come into their powers they'll be extinct. Voice from the back: "Don't count on it, sister."

Meanwhile, back at the Ivory Tower, a woman rings me up from a fashion magazine soliciting my opinion on female bodily hair, and a man asks me to read to at some conference of north Americans for free (for the *exposure* and besides I might even get some *travel opportunity*). I tell the woman the Irish public can probably survive without my deep thoughts; I tell the man the Union takes a dim view of writers working for nothing – try asking a plumber to fix your toilet for the *exposure*.

I go searching out the ghost of my younger self. She came through the gates as a seventeen year old student sure she could change the world – like immediately. It's taken her the best part of twenty years to even begin to change herself. Her world was black and white; the goodies and the baddies instantly recognizable. How would she cope with the fog I move in? The night of the Trinity Ball, I print off the computer the poems I've made in the months in residence. Scenes of Dionysian abandon outside the windows, lovers wrapped around each other or tearing each other apart, hot salsa from the Dining Hall steps, ten thousand ravers with as many states of consciousness, mostly chemically induced. I offer her the new poems terrified of her clear gaze, her simple world.

Darren Donohue

THE BELL-RINGERS

Taking hold of the sally
with knowledgeable hands,
feet apart,
facing inward,
circled and focused,
they prepare
to conjure a storm of iron.
Arms pull
and the rope drops,
racing to the bottom
of silence.

Sliver-tongued tulips
toss their heads
and bellow thunder,
cornered dust jumps
and glitters. Beneath
the bell-ringers' heave
stained glass Saints
rattle their frames.

Oh to be circled there,
gripping time by the throat,
lassoing and
taming its final secret.
Starved of context,
I can only wrench upon
these words,
waiting patiently
as a lightning rod
for Arcadia to arrive
and strike this page.

Eugene Platt

MUSING AT THE MUSIC BARN

In a far corner of Charleston's liveliest venue,
where shyness and acne have relegated me,
my seat shakes with vibrations of a Mersey beat.

My body moves in imitation
of the undulations of foreign bodies
as I, a minor, cuddle a forbidden beer.

I search their chirpy sounds
and follow their famous faces to see
if there is any way we may be related.

I decide, that in a shared desire to create,
even if not born and bred brothers,
we are at least kindred spirits,

and far enough removed so that
effusive fan mail could be sent
without fear of embarrassment.

Hearing this heralded band from England
beats dancing at the high school sock hop
where my mom gullibly believes me to be.

By the time I get home, she's sure to be asleep
or at least too tired to question me tonight –
and I need to write those lads from Liverpool.

Meanwhile, music communicates,
though as the poet John Donne wrote,
'more than kisses, letters mingle souls'.

Angela Finn

BURNOUT

Young girls we dragged
on slim cigarettes, feigned British accents
laughed at ourselves, dictated letters;
Dear Mr So and So, My husband and I ...
Our notional spouses were sophisticated,
wore elegant suits, Eton shirts, were mostly absent.

Decades later, a summer evening,
I ask if she remembers any of this.
We are inside The Cedar Tree eating
tabbouleh, sharing a bottle of house red.
She blinks, shakes her head no –
a memory lapse I put down to lithium,

isolation, a heartbreak down under.
She is eager suddenly to talk
about her first vision on the way
to a barbecue, riding pillion passenger
on her fiancé's Harley; he could not see
the orange flames dancing behind the mountains.

The waiter takes our empty plates. I ask
if she remembers the bedsit we shared,
the James Bond bed that folded into the wall,
remember? Tufnell Park, late 1980s?
Remember the Italian landlord, the kitchenette
across the landing, the sliding door?

Magnolia walls? Her finger circles the rim of glass,
she says she's amazed I remember
such detail. I tell her about the night
we almost set the place on fire, a candle
left burning beneath the bookshelf, how
we hoped the landlord wouldn't notice

the charring, the painted-over black patches.
She doesn't, but recalls being alone
in India, threatened; all those men wanted
was warm women and cold beer, she says.

This life has deformed us: psychosis,
divorce, melted dreams, contortions.

Between courses we step outside for
a cigarette, air, the streets loud
with Friday-night laughter, drunkenness,
cluelessness. Between the rooftops
the pink and orange sky darkening,
forgotten-about stars re-emerging.

Notes on Contributors

Deborah Bacharach is the author of *After I Stop Lying* (Cherry Grove Collections, 2015). Her poems and essays have been published in journals nationally and internationally, including *The Moth, The Antigonish Review, Arts & Letters, Calyx, Cimarron Review, New Letters, Poet Lore*, and in the anthology *A Fierce Brightness: Twenty-Five Years of Women's Poetry*.

Charlie Bondhus is the author of *Divining Bones* (Sundress, 2018) and *All the Heat We Could Carry* (Main Street Rag, 2013), winner of the Thom Gunn Award for Gay Poetry. He received his MFA in creative writing from Goddard College and his Ph.D. in literature from UMASS Amherst. His work has appeared in *Poetry, The Missouri Review, Columbia Journal, Hayden's Ferry Review, Bellevue Literary Review, Nimrod*, and *Copper Nickel*. He is associate professor of English at Raritan Valley Community College (NJ).

Colette Bryce's *Selected Poems* won the Pigott Poetry Prize in 2018. A new collection, *The M Pages*, is forthcoming in 2020.

Paddy Bushe, born in Dublin in 1948, now lives in Kerry. He is a poet, editor, and translator in both Irish and English. Two collections, *Peripheral Vision* and *Second Sight*, a dual-language selection of his poems in Irish, will be published by Dedalus Press in early 2020. He is a member of Aosdána, and Artistic Director of The Amergin Solstice Poetry Gathering.

Chad Campbell is the author of *Laws & Locks* (Signal Editions, 2015) and the chapbook *Euphonia* (Anstruther Press, 2017). A graduate of the Iowa Writers' Workshop, he is currently a doctoral candidate at The University of Manchester's Centre for New Writing. His second book, *The Night Field*, is forthcoming from Signal Editions in 2020.

Siobhán Campbell's latest collection is *Heat Signature* (Seren Press, 2017). She is a contributor to *Making Integral: Critical Essays on Richard Murphy* (Cork University Press, 2019), and is on faculty at The Open University. Recent work appears in *Open-Eyed, Full-Throated: An Anthology of American/Irish Poets* (Arlen House, 2019).

Moya Cannon's most recent collection is *Keats Lives* (Carcanet Press, 2015). She has received the Brendan Behan Award and the O'Shaughnessy Award, and was Heimbold Professor of Irish Studies at Villanova University in 2011. She has edited *Poetry Ireland Review* and is a member of Aosdána. Her sixth collection, *Donegal Tarantella*, is forthcoming from Carcanet Press.

Joe Carrick-Varty's poems have appeared in *Magma Poetry, PN Review,* and *The Dark Horse*. In 2018 he won the New Poets Prize, and in 2019 he was selected by Martina Evans for the Poetry Ireland Introductions Readings. His debut pamphlet *Somewhere Far* is published by The Poetry Business.

Ciaran Carson's lives with his family in Belfast. The Gallery Press published *From There to Here: Selected Poems and Translations* last October on the occasion of his 70th birthday, and will publish *Still Life* (new poems) on 16 October 2019.

Catriona Clutterbuck's publication credits include *Cyphers, Oxford Poetry, The Blue Nib, The Honest Ulsterman, Oxford Poets 2007: An Anthology, The May Anthology of Oxford and Cambridge Poetry* (1993), and *Women's Work*. A chapbook, *Ghosts in my Heels*, was published in 2005. She was selected for the Poetry Ireland Introductions Readings in 2006. She lives in Co Tipperary.

A.M. Cousins' publication credits include *Poetry Ireland Review, The Stinging Fly*, and online at the Poethead archive. Her work was highly commended in The Patrick Kavanagh Poetry Award in 2015 and 2016, and she featured in the Poetry Ireland Introductions Readings in 2016. She is working on a first collection of poetry, and writes for *Sunday Miscellany*.

Bernie Crawford lives near the sea in Oranmore, Co Galway. She won second place in the Blue Nib Chapbook Summer 2018 competition, and first prize in the 2017 Trócaire Poetry Ireland Competition. Her poetry has been featured on *Sunday Miscellany* and has been published in *The North, The Stony Thursday Book, Mslexia, Crannóg* and elsewhere. She is on the editorial board of *Skylight 47*, and is working on her first collection.

Jonathan C Creasy is a writer, musician, broadcaster, and educator based in Dublin. He is editor-in-chief and publisher at New Dublin Press, producer and presenter of *The Writers' Room*, and an IRC fellow in University College Dublin, where he lectures in English and Creative Writing.

Christopher Cusack is an academic and writer living in Nijmegen, the Netherlands. His critical and literary writing has appeared in the *Times Literary Supplement, The Irish Times, Banshee*, and *Poetry Salzburg Review.*

Colin Dardis is a poet, editor, and arts facilitator. His latest collection is *The Dogs of Humanity* (Fly on the Wall Poetry, 2019).

Iulia David is a Romanian-born, London-based poet who graduated from the MA in Writing Poetry at the Poetry School and Newcastle University. Her work has been published or is forthcoming in *Magma, The Rialto, harana poetry, Perverse,* and the League Against Cruel Sports anthology, *For the Silent*.

Steve Denehan's recent publication credits include *The Irish Times, The Phoenix, The Blue Nib, The Opiate, The Hungry Chimera, Evening Street Review, Ink In Thirds, Crack the Spine,* and *The Cape Rock*. He has been nominated for The Pushcart Prize, and his chapbook, *Of Thunder, Pearls and Birdsong*, is available from Fowlpox Press. He lives in Kildare.

Darren Donohue's poetry is published in *The Irish Times, Irish Independent, Cyphers, Sixteen Magazine, Rebel Poetry, The Best of Vine Leaves*, and *The Poetry Box*. In 2017, he read for the Poetry Ireland Introduction Series, and he is currently writer-in-residence at Carlow College, St Patrick's.

Katie Donovan has published five collections of poetry, all with Bloodaxe Books, most recently *Off Duty*, shortlisted for the Poetry Now Award. She received the O'Shaughnessy Award in 2017, and has taught Creative Writing at NUI Maynooth and at IADT, Dún Laoghaire. Her work is widely anthologised, notably in the best-selling *Staying Alive: Real Poems for Unreal Times* (Bloodaxe Books).

Berni Dwan's first poetry collection, *Frankly, Baby*, is published by Lapwing Publications (2018). Her work has appeared in *The Galway Review, The Irish Times, Crannóg, A New Ulster, The Rose Magazine, FLARE*, and elsewhere. She was shortlisted for the Anthony Cronin International Poetry Award in 2019. Her one-woman poetry show, *Unrhymed Dublin*, was accepted for inclusion in the 2016 Scene + Heard Festival at Smock Alley Theatre.

Martin Dyar won the Patrick Kavanagh Poetry Award in 2009. His first book of poems, *Maiden Names* (Arlen House) was shortlisted for the Pigott Poetry Prize. He is the editor of an anthology of poems on medical subjects, which will be published by Poetry Ireland in Autumn 2020.

Gary Egan has published in Ireland (*Irish Examiner, U magazine*), the UK (*Chapman, The New Writer*), the US (*Suddenly Lost in Words, Verbatim, The Language Quarterly*), and Australia (*Famous Reporter, Island*). He has also performed stand-up tragedy on The Giraffe's Neck Tour at a variety of locations, including the dingleberries of The Edinburgh Fringe.

Nidhi Zak/Aria Eipe's poems are published/forthcoming in literary journals including *Acorn, ARDOR, Banshee, B O D Y, Rattle, Splonk*, and *The Irish Times*, and featured in interactive installations such as *Raining Poetry* and *Poetry Jukebox* in Dublin. A recipient of an inaugural Ireland Chair of Poetry Student Prize, her work was selected for the Cork International Poetry Festival's Introductions Series 2019 and won a First Book Club Award at the Jaipur Literature Festival 2018.

Rebecca Farmer was born in Birmingham, though both her parents come from Dublin. Her poems have been widely published. In 2014 her pamphlet *Not Really* was an overall winner in The Poetry Business International Book & Pamphlet Competition. In 2019 she was awarded second prize in the Strokestown International Poetry Competition. She recently completed a Ph.D. in Creative Writing at Goldsmiths, where her critical thesis was on the later poems of Louis MacNeice and his work at the BBC.

Angela Finn was selected for the Poetry Ireland Introductions Readings in 2019. She was nominated for a 2018 Hennessy New Irish Writing Award (Emerging Fiction). Her writing has appeared in *The Irish Times*, the *Fish Anthology*, *New Planet Cabaret* (New Island Press), and elsewhere.

Matthew Geden was born and brought up in the English Midlands, moving to Kinsale in 1990. His most recent collection is *The Place Inside*, published by Dedalus Press.

Regan Good is a poet living in Brooklyn, New York. Her first book, *The Atlantic House*, was published in 2011. Her second book, *The Needle*, will be published this autumn. She is currently working on a book of poems that takes inspiration from the landscapes of Orkney, Northumberland and the now submerged mesolithic landscape known as Doggerland.

Philip Gross has published some twenty collections of poetry, including *A Bright Acoustic* (Bloodaxe Books, 2017), winning the TS Eliot Prize in 2009, and a Cholmondeley Award in 2017. He is a keen collaborator – with artist Valerie Coffin Price on A *Fold In The River* (Seren, 2015), and with poet Lesley Saunders on *A Part of the Main* (Mulfran, 2018). His science-based collection for young people, *Dark Sky Park* (Otter-Barry Books, 2018), is shortlisted for the CLiPPA award, 2019.

Alison Hackett is the founder of publishing house 21st Century Renaissance, and author of *The Visual Time Traveller: 500 Years of History, Art and Science in 100 Unique Designs*, selected for the Global Irish Design Challenge exhibition in 2016. In 2017 she published *Crabbing* (poetry) and *Yours etc: Letters printed in Irish and British papers, 2010–2017*.

Rachael Hegarty was born in Dublin and reared in Finglas. Her debut collection, *Flight Paths Over Finglas*, won the 2018 Shine / Strong Award. Her collection *May Day 1974* was published this year by Salmon Poetry.

Eva Isherwood-Wallace recently completed an MA in Poetry at the Seamus Heaney Centre, Queen's University Belfast. She was highly commended in Christ Church College, Oxford's The Tower Poetry Competition 2013, and was shortlisted for the New Voices award in UCD's Voices of War International Poetry Competition 2018. Her work is published in *The Tangerine* and *Banshee*.

Rosie Jackson lives near Frome, Somerset. *What the Ground Holds* (Poetry Salzburg, 2014) was followed by *The Light Box* (Cultured Llama, 2016) and her memoir *The Glass Mother* (Unthank, 2016). Rosie has taught at the University of East Anglia, UWE, and Cortijo Romero, Spain. She won first prize in the Stanley Spencer Poetry competition 2017. *Two Girls and a Beehive* (poems about Spencer, a collaboration with Graham Burchell) will be published by Two Rivers Press in 2020.

Fred Johnston received a Prix de l'Ambassade for work on translations in 2002, and in 2004 he was writer-in-residence with the Princess Grace Irish Library at Monaco. His latest collection of poetry is *Rogue States* (Salmon Poetry, 2018). He lives in Galway.

Virginia Keane was born in 1945 and grew up in Ardmore, Co Waterford, with her mother, Molly Keane, the novelist, and her sister Sally Phipps. She is now a director of The Molly Keane Writers' Retreat in Ardmore. She has always written but has only began to work seriously on poetry since the Molly Keane Writers' Retreat started ten years ago. *POETRY* (Chicago) published one of her poems in 2018.

Benjamin Keatinge is a Visiting Research Fellow at the School of English, Trinity College Dublin. He has edited *Making Integral: Critical Essays on Richard Murphy* (Cork University Press, 2019). From 2007 to 2016 he worked as Associate Professor of English at South East European University, Macedonia. Based in Ireland, he divides his time between Dublin and Skopje.

Susan Kelly is from Westport, Co Mayo. Her work has appeared in *Cyphers, Poetry Ireland Review, Crannóg, Revival, Abridged, The London Magazine, Boyne Berries, Burning Bush* 2, and *wordlegs*. She was a featured reader at Over the Edge in Galway (2011), shortlisted for the Over the Edge New Writer of the Year (2013), and longlisted for the WOW! award (2014).

Sophie Klahr is the author of *Meet Me Here At Dawn* (YesYes Books, 2016) and the chapbook _____ *Versus Recovery* (Pilot Books). Her poetry appears or is forthcoming in *The New Yorker, American Poetry Review, Poetry London,* and other publications. Recently a Philip Roth Resident at the Stadler Centre for Poetry and Literary Arts, she is the 2019/20 Kenan Visiting Writer at UNC-Chapel Hill.

Joanna Klink is the author of four books of poetry. Her poems appear in many anthologies, including *Resistance, Rebellion, Life: 50 Poems Now,* and *The Penguin Anthology of Twentieth Century American Poetry.* She has received awards and fellowships from the Rona Jaffe Foundation, the American Academy of Arts and Letters, the Trust of Amy Lowell, and the Guggenheim Foundation. Joanna teaches in the MFA Program at the University of Montana. Her new book is forthcoming in 2020.

Camilla Lambert's pamphlet *Grapes in the Crater* was published by Indigo Dreams Publishing in 2015, and she is currently working on a new collection. Individual poems have appeared in *Acumen, Agenda, The Frogmore Papers, The Interpreter's House, SOUTH* (profiled poet April 2017), and in various anthologies. She co-organises a small arts festival in Binsted, near Arundel, West Sussex, which includes running a nationally advertised poetry competition, from which an anthology is produced.

Ann Leahy's first collection, *The Woman who Lived her Life Backwards* (Arlen House), won the Patrick Kavanagh Poetry Award. In 2018, she was amongst the winners of the Troubadour International Prize and was shortlisted for the Shirley McClure Prize, Los Gatos, California. Her poems have been commended in the National Poetry Competition (UK).

Pippa Little is Scots and lives in Northumberland. She is a reviewer, editor, workshop facilitator, and mentor, and has been a Royal Literary Fund Fellow at Newcastle University School of English for the past five years. Her second collection *Twist*, from Arc Publications, was shortlisted for the Saltire Scottish Poetry Book of the Year, and she is currently working on a third. 'The Afternoon War Ends' was shortlisted in the Voices of War Poetry Competition run by UCD.

Tá dánta le Marcus Mac Conghail foilsithe sna bailiúcháin *If Ever You Go* agus *Calling Cards*. Tá dánta ráite aige i gcúig chúige na hÉireann. Is ceoltóir agus cumadóir amhrán é leis agus le déanaí bhí sé ag buaileadh ceoil i nGaoth Dobhair agus ar Árainn Mhór le Thatchers of the Acropolis.

Caoimhín Mac Giolla Léith teaches in the School of Irish, Celtic Studies, and Folklore at University College Dublin. He has published extensively on literature in the Irish language, both medieval and modern, and on contemporary art.

Richie McCaffery lives in Alnwick, Northumberland. He holds a Ph.D. in Scottish literature from the University of Glasgow, and is the author of two pamphlet collections of poems as well as two book length collections, *Cairn* (2014) and *Passport* (2018), both from Nine Arches Press. In 2018 he co-edited, with Alistair Peebles, *The Tiny Talent: Selected Poems of Joan Ure* (Brae Editions). He is busy working on his third pamphlet.

Jaki McCarrick is an award-winning writer of plays, poetry, and fiction. Her debut story collection *The Scattering* (Seren Books) was shortlisted for the 2014 Edge Hill Prize and she has had international success with her play, *Belfast Girls*. Her poems have been published in numerous literary journals and she regularly writes for the *Times Literary Supplement*.

Paul McCarrick holds an MA in Writing from NUI Galway. He has been published in *The Blue Nib*, *Crannóg*, *The Stinging Fly*, and elsewhere. He was selected for the 2019 Poetry Ireland Introductions Readings. He has also received an Arts Bursary from Westmeath County Arts Office. He lives in Athlone, Co Westmeath where he is completing his first collection.

Ian Maleney is a writer from Offaly, currently living in Dublin. *Minor Monuments*, a collection of essays, is published by Tramp Press (2019).

Lorraine Mariner has published two collections with Picador, *Furniture* (2009), which was shortlisted for the Seamus Heaney Centre First Collection Poetry Prize, and *There Will Be No More Nonsense* (2014). She has a pamphlet forthcoming with Grey Suit Editions.

Paula Meehan was Ireland Professor of Poetry, 2013-2016. Her latest collection is *Geomantic* (Dedalus Press, 2016).

Kate Miller's book *The Observances* (2015), shortlisted for the Costa Book Award for Poetry, won the Seamus Heaney Centre First Collection Poetry Prize. Her second collection is due from Carcanet Press in 2020.

David Murphy's poetry has been published in magazines and anthologies in Ireland and abroad, including *The Poetry Bus, The Stony Thursday Book, Revival, Burning Bush 2, Irish Literary Review, Cyphers, The Ogham Stone, The Stinging Fly* and *THE SHOp*. The poem 'Bolivia' won a prize at the 2018 Red Line Book Festival.

Caitlin Newby – see page 115.

Colette Nic Aodha, based in Galway, is an award-winning poet and fiction writer, in both Irish and English. Her fourteen publications include one volume of English poetry, *Sundial*, published by Arlen House, and two dual-language poetry collections with the same publisher; *Between Curses: Bainne Géar*, and *In Castlewood: An Ghaoth Aduaidh*. Her collected poems (bilingual) is titled *Bainne Géar: Spoilt Milk* (Arlen House, 2016).

File sa dá theanga í **Dairena Ní Chinnéide**. I measc naoi gcnuasach foilsithe aici tá *Fé Gheasa: Spellbound* (Arlen House, 2016), *Cloithear Aistear Anama* (Coiscéim, 2013), agus *An Trodaí & Dánta Eile / The Warrior & Other Poems* (Cló Iar Chonnacht, 2006). Tá a céad cnuasach Béarla, *DELETED*, á fhoilsiú go luath ag Salmon Poetry.

Laoighseach Ní Choistealbha is an Irish Research Council Laureate Scholar in NUI Galway, working as part of the project 'Republic of Conscience: Human Rights and Modern Irish Poetry'. She is also a poet and has been published in *Comhar* and *Feasta*.

CL O'Dell's poems have appeared or are forthcoming in *The New Yorker, Poetry, Ploughshares, New England Review, Best New Poets*, and elsewhere. He lives in the Hudson Valley and is editor of *The Paris-American*.

Grace O'Doherty is from Co Wicklow and lives in Lisbon. Her poetry has been published in *The Honest Ulsterman, Banshee*, and *The Stony Thursday Poetry Anthology*. She performed at the Spotlight on New Voices event at Cúirt International Festival of Literature 2018, and was a recipient of the Sylvia O'Brien Prize.

Patrick O'Donnell is originally from Donegal. After meeting his wife in England, he settled in Kilkenny. 'Annie', in this issue of *Poetry Ireland Review*, is his first published poem.

Kevin O'Farrell is a poet and artist from Dublin. He is working towards a first collection.

Pádraig Ó Tuama's books include *Readings from the Book of Exile* and *Sorry for Your Troubles*. His poems have appeared in *Image Journal*, AAP's poem-a-day, and have been broadcast on RTÉ, NPR, and the BBC. Born in Cork, he now lives in Belfast.

Eugene Platt, an octogenarian, grew up in the Lowcountry of South Carolina. His first collection, *Coffee and Solace*, was published in 1970 while studying at Trinity College Dublin. (Brendan Kennelly allowed him to sell copies at the front gate). Subsequent collections include *An Original Sin* (Briarpatch Press). His poems have appeared in various publications including *Icarus*, *Capella*, *Poet Lore*, *Tar River Poetry*, *The South Carolina Review*, and *Ireland of the Welcomes*. He has given over 100 public readings of his work, and read in the inaugural Dublin Arts Festival.

Laura Potts, twice-recipient of the Foyle Young Poets of the Year Award, became one of the BBC's New Voices last year. Her first BBC radio drama aired at Christmas. She was nominated for The Pushcart Prize and received a commendation from The Poetry Society in 2018.

Liz Quirke, originally from Tralee, lives in Spiddal, Co Galway with her wife and daughters. After a decade in journalism and television production, Liz is now in the second year of a Ph.D. in Creative Practice – Poetry. Salmon Poetry published her debut collection, *The Road, Slowly*, in 2018.

James Ragan has published nine books of poetry, with work appearing in *Poetry*, *The Nation*, *Los Angeles Times*, *World Literature Today*, and in many anthologies. Honours include three Fulbright Professorships, two Honorary Ph.D.'s, the Emerson Poetry Prize, nine Pushcart nominations, an NEA grant, the Swan Foundation Humanitarian Award, and the Platinum Remi Award at the Houston International Film Festival, as the subject of the documentary *Flowers and Roots: Ambassador of the Arts*.

Andrew Rahal's chapbook *No New Wilderness* was a finalist for the Gertrude Press Poetry Prize and the Cathexis Northwest Press Chapbook Contest. He was selected for the 2019 Poetry Ireland Introductions Readings. He is an Assistant Poetry Editor at *Narrative* Magazine and a Ph.D. student at the Seamus Heaney Centre at Queen's University, where he is the recipient of a 2018 AHSS International Faculty Award.

Eoin Rogers is a graduate of the NUI Galway MA in Writing programme. In 2018 he was selected for the Cúirt International Festival of Literature Poetry Mentorship Programme. He lives in Dublin.

Grace Smith has lived most of her life in Dublin. 'Sestina for Red Shoes', in this issue of *Poetry Ireland Review*, is her first published poem.

Larry Stapleton's poetry has been published previously in *Poetry Ireland Review* and has also appeared in *The Stinging Fly, THE SHOp, Cyphers, The Stony Thursday Book, Crannóg, The Honest Ulsterman, The North, The Interpreter's House, Irish Pages*, and in *The Irish Times*.

Anthony Walton is the author of *Mississippi: An American Journey*, and the editor, with Michael S Harper, of *The Vintage Book of African American Poetry* and *Every Shut-Eye Ain't Asleep: An Anthology of Poetry by African Americans Since 1945*. His poems have appeared in *The New Yorker, Black Scholar, Oxford American, Notre Dame Review*, and *Kenyon Review*, among many other magazines and journals.

JS Watts is a poet and novelist. Her poetry, short stories and non-fiction appear in publications in Britain, Ireland, Canada, Australia and America including *Acumen, Envoi, Mslexia*, and *Orbis*, and have been broadcast on BBC and independent radio. Her published books include: *Cats and Other Myths, Songs of Steelyard Sue, Years Ago You Coloured Me, The Submerged Sea* (poetry) and *A Darker Moon* and *Witchlight* (novels).

Grace Wilentz is a poet, reviewer, and teacher based in the Liberties, Dublin. Her debut pamphlet, *Holding Distance*, will be published by Green Bottle Press in Autumn 2019.

Erin Wilson's poems have appeared in or are forthcoming in *Kestrel, A Journal of Literature and Art, The American Journal of Poetry, The Adirondack Review, Natural Bridge, The Curlew*, and others. She lives and writes in a small town in northern Ontario, Canada.

Glen Wilson is a civil servant and Worship Leader at St Mark's Church of Ireland, Portadown. He studied English and Politics at Queen's University Belfast. He is widely published, having work in *The Honest Ulsterman, Iota, The Paperclip*, and other journals. He won the Seamus Heaney Award for New Writing in 2017, and the Jonathan Swift Creative Writing Award in 2018. His first collection of poetry is *An Experience on the Tongue* (Doire Press, 2019).